GRACIOUS VOICES

•

Shouts
and
Whispers
for
God
Seekers

compiled
and
edited
by

William P.
McDonald

DISCIPLESHIP RESOURCES

MATERIALS FOR GROWTH IN CHRISTIAN FAITH & LIFE

— NASHVILLE, TENNESSEE —

P.O. Box 840 • Nashville, TN 37202-0840

Library of Congress Catalog Card No. 96-86581

ISBN 0-88177-178-3

DR178

Gracious Voices

TABLE OF CONTENTS

THE LORD'S PRAYER

Initiation: Joined to Christ and the Church

Gracious Voices

This book is to introduce you, the seeker, to a chorus of gracious voices—saints, martyrs, theologians, hymn writers, preachers, poets, mystics, prophets, reformers, renewers, ordinary folk—who will accompany you on the journey to baptism and church membership. It may be read in group settings under the guidance of leaders, or alone as a guide to prayer and meditation. In either context, you will discover something of what discipleship is about.

Being a disciple is being part of the church, which is more than just the local congregation, conference, or denomination. Even Christians of every stripe present in the world today do not exhaust what it means to be *church*. We believe in the universal church, which means participating in a great communion of believers across time and space, who depend on one another and expect one another to remain faithful to the cross and resurrection of Jesus Christ. When you enter the church, you enter into fellowship not only with the local church or denomination, but with all the redeemed of every time and place, united in a common bond of baptismal faith, diversely expressed and practiced. These are your mothers, fathers, sisters, and brothers in faith who have passed on to you their agonies, their prayers and praises, their questions and their bold affirmations, in trust that the same Holy Spirit which guided them will lead you in joining your voice and your story with theirs.

Becoming part of the church is like being invited to a meal. With this book in hand, imagine that a generous plate of food is passed down a great banquet table to you. The stories and adventures of fellow pilgrims from past and present are being served to you, so that you may sing and struggle with them and finally affirm with them the graciousness of the table's host, our Lord himself.

The food which is being passed down the table to you may taste very different from your usual fare. Some is contemporary. Other comes from long ago and far away. Many of the men and women who wrote or spoke them did not share current sensibilities or sensitivities. For that reason their words and thoughts may sound strange to us. Even the spelling, which has been retained as originally written, may seem odd. Yet, from their minds and hearts come gracious words. Theirs are gracious words for us, not because we like them, are soothed by them, or agree with them at every turn. Their voices are gracious because these men and women experienced the grace, majesty, mystery, and transforming power of the triune God they knew and proclaimed in Jesus Christ. They knew God in their own time and place, as we must know and proclaim this God known in Christ in our time and place.

Nonetheless, you will find their fare to be hearty food that must be broken off, chewed, swallowed, and digested before it can nourish. Some readings in this book may take time to understand and appreciate. You are invited to mull over them, struggle with them, and share them with others on the journey with you. This is no baby food. It is not milk for infants. These voices are meat for people whom God is calling to faith and conversion.

Think of this book as a journal in which other Christians have recorded their words about what their faith journey with the church means. All of them present the church's basic affirmations of faith. Some are straightforward and plain. Others are quite provocative. For instance, you might be struck by what others have said about searching out God's call in the first section, on inquiry, and find you are sharing much the same search as some Christian from a distant time and place. Or, the entries in the section on the Lord's Prayer might uncover for you the hidden treasure in its simple words. Hence, the margins of the pages invite you to jot down your thoughts. As you write, you are learning to put that same faith shared with believers across the ages into words that are genuinely your own. *Gracious Voices* becomes your journal as you learn to tune your voice to the chorus in the way God is calling you.

The book is arranged according to the stages of the Christian Initiation process outlined in *Come to the Waters.* The readings may be used in discussions at appropriate times from inquiry to initiation. The enrollment period covers the weeks of Advent or Lent, during which time candidates for initiation in the early church were often taught the Creed and the Lord's Prayer. The selections for each creedal article and prayer petition provide opportunity to reflect on the meaning of these monuments of the faith and to hear and pray the basic affirmations of the Christian faith, with a Wesleyan accent. May each gracious voice supply challenge and affirmation as you journey to the waters of the font.

William P. McDonald
Easter 1996

Gracious Voices

As a deer longs for flowing streams,
  so my soul longs for you, O God.

Psalm 42:1

You move us to delight in praising You; for You have made us for
Yourself, and our hearts are restless till they find rest in You.

Augustine, 354-430, North Africa

Come, sinners, to the gospel feast; let every soul be Jesus' guest.
Ye need not one be left behind, for God hath bid all humankind.

Sent by my Lord, on you I call; the invitation is to all.
Come, all the world! Come, sinner, thou!
All things in Christ are ready now.

Come, all ye souls, by sin oppressed, ye restless wanderers after rest;
ye poor, and maimed, and halt, and blind,
in Christ a hearty welcome find.

My message as from God receive; ye all may come to Christ and live.
O let his love your hearts constrain, nor suffer him to die in vain.

This is the time, no more delay! This is the Lord's accepted day.
Come thou, this moment, at his call,
and live for him who died for all.

Charles Wesley, 1707-1788, England

Go from your country and your kindred and your father's house
to the land that I will show you.

Genesis 12:1

O Lord my God,
teach my heart where and how to seek you,
where and how to find you.
Lord, if you are not here but absent,
where shall I seek you?
But you are everywhere, so you must be here,
why then do I not seek you?

Anselm, 1033?-1109, England

The Lord pursued me for a long time. He put me, as it were, into
prison in order to force me to contemplate him and speak to him.
He deprived me of everything that I might go and prostrate myself
at his feet; but invariably I again attached myself to nothingness in
order to shun the abyss of love that Jesus had in store for me.

attributed to Peter Julian Eymard, 1811-1868, France

Do not be astonished that I said to you, "You must be born from above." The wind blows where it chooses, and you hear the sound of it, but you do not know where it comes from or where it goes. So it is with everyone who is born of the Spirit.

John 3:7-8

Lord, you have come to the lakeshore
looking neither for wealthy nor wise ones;
you only asked me to follow humbly.
O Lord, with your eyes you have searched me,
and while smiling have spoken my name;
now my boat's left on the shoreline behind me;
by your side I will seek other seas.

Cesareo Gabarain, 1936-1991, Spain

Have you ever been up late watching TV and felt drawn to the refrigerator? You open the door and stare absently inside while the cold rushes out at your feet. You don't know what will be satisfying, but finally pick out something to eat. In a few minutes you are back in the kitchen to get something to drink, thinking that was what you wanted all along. At last you are full—too full—and realize you weren't really hungry or thirsty after all.

The first stage in the journey of spiritual growth is something like that. But instead of the hunger being physical, it is a hunger of the heart. Many people ignore this crucial moment of awakening because they do not understand what is happening to them. It is a stage that can be both distressing and depressing because no matter what we do, our life just isn't what we once thought it was meant to be. Confusion. Unrest. Dissatisfaction. These are but three of the most common feelings at this time. . . .

Often the hunger of the heart is experienced as the desire to get something more *out* of life. While there's nothing wrong with that, the hunger of the heart is really a reminder to bring something more *into* life. That something more is an ongoing relationship with God and an ever-deepening faith.

Ron DelBene, United States

For some time past I had indulged the fancy of offering myself up to the Child Jesus as a plaything, for him to do what he liked with me. I don't mean an expensive plaything; give a child an expensive toy and he will sit looking at it without daring to touch it. But a toy of no value—a ball, say—is at his disposal; he can throw it to the ground, kick it about, make a hole in it, leave it lying in a corner, or press it to his heart if he feels that way about it.

Thérèse de Lisieux, 1873-1897, France

Gracious Voices

Come, all of you, come, men and women,
come forward, drink of the water provided for you;
all of you who are thirsty, come to me to drink
from the water of life, provided by Jesus your Lord.

Laotian Hymn, translated by Cher Lue Vang

Whoever wishes for God alone is rich in every good. Happy the
one who can say: "My Jesus, I desire thee alone, and nothing more!"

Alphonsus Liguori, 1696-1787, Italy

You have loved us first, O God, alas! We speak of it in terms of
history as if You have only loved us first but a single time, rather
than without ceasing. You have loved us first many times and every
day and our whole life through. When we wake up in the morning
and turn our soul toward You—You are the first—You have loved us
first; If I rise at dawn and at the same second turn my soul toward
You in prayer, You are there ahead of me, You have loved me first.
When I withdraw from the distractions of the day and turn my soul
toward You, You are the first and thus forever. And yet we always
speak ungratefully as if You have loved us only once.

Søren Kierkegaard, 1813-1855, Denmark

I believe, O Lord, that Thou hast not abandoned me to the dim
light of my own reason to conduct me to happiness, but that Thou
hast revealed in the Holy Scriptures whatever is necessary for me
to believe and practice, in order to my eternal salvation.

Richard Allen, 1760-1831, United States

Thou hidden love of God, whose height,
  whose depth unfathomed no one knows,
I see from far thy beauteous light,
  and inly sigh for thy repose;
my heart is pained, nor can it be
  at rest, till it finds rest in thee.

'Tis mercy all that thou hast brought
  my mind to seek its peace in thee;
yet while I seek, but find thee not,
  no peace my wandering soul shall see.
O when shall all my wanderings end,
  and all my steps to theeward tend?

Gerhard Tersteegen, 1697-1769, Germany

Thirst
for
Jesus,
so that
he may
inebriate
you with
his love.

Isaac of
Nineveh,
seventh
century,
East Syria

The old men used to say, "When you see a young man ascending up to heaven through his own will, seize him by the foot and pull him down, for this is good for him."

a saying of the Desert Fathers, fourth century, Syria/Palestine/Egypt

Here there begins an eternal hunger, which shall never more be satisfied; it is an inward craving and yearning of the created spirit for the loving power of an uncreated God. And since the spirit longs for fruition and is invited and urged thereto by God, it must continually desire its fulfillment. Behold, now begins an eternal craving and insatiable longing.

Jan Van Ruysbroeck, 1293?-1381, Holland

Grace strikes us when we are in great pain and restlessness. It strikes us when we walk through the dark valley of a meaningless and empty life. It shakes us when we feel that our separation is deeper than usual.

Paul Tillich, 1886-1965, Germany/United States

God showed me too the pleasure it gives him when a simple soul comes to him, openly, sincerely, and genuinely.

Julian of Norwich, 1342?-?, England

Come to me, all you that are weary and are carrying heavy burdens, and I will give you rest. Take my yoke upon you, and learn from me; for I am gentle and humble in heart, and you will find rest for your souls. For my yoke is easy, and my burden is light.

Matthew 11:28-30

I am bold in saying this, but I believe that no one is ever changed, either by doctrine, by hearing the Word, or by preaching or teaching of another, unless the affections are moved by these things. No one ever seeks salvation, no one ever cries for wisdom, no one ever wrestles with God, no one ever kneels in prayer or flees from sin, with a heart that remains unaffected. In a word, there is never any great achievement by the things of religion without a heart deeply affected by those things.

Jonathan Edwards, 1703-1758, New England

Gracious Voices

We acknowledge God's prevenient grace, the divine love that surrounds all humanity and precedes any and all of our conscious impulses. This grace prompts our first wish to please God, our first glimmer of understanding concerning God's will, and our "first slight transient conviction" of having sinned against God.

The Book of Discipline of The United Methodist Church, 1992

Conscience . . . Can it be denied that something of this is found in everyone born into the world? And does it not appear as soon as the understanding opens, as soon as reason begins to wan? Does not every one then begin to know that there is a difference between good and evil; how imperfect soever the various circumstances of this sense of good and evil may be? Does not every man, for instance, know, unless blinded by the prejudices of education, . . . that it is good to honour his parents? Do not all men, however uneducated and barbarous, allow, it is right to do to others as we would have them do to us? And are not all who know this condemned in their own mind when they do anything contrary thereto? as, on the other hand, when they act suitable thereto, they have the approbation of their own conscience?

This faculty seems to be what is usually meant by those who speak of natural conscience; an expression frequently found in some of our best authors, but yet not strictly just. For though in one sense it may be termed natural, because it is found in all men; yet, properly speaking, it is not natural, but a supernatural gift of God, above all his natural endowments. No; it is not nature, but the Son of God, that is "the true light, which enlighteneth every man that cometh into the world." So that we may say to every human creature, "God," not nature, "hath showed thee, O mortal, what is good." And it is his Spirit who giveth thee an inward check, who causeth thee to feel uneasy, when thou walkest in any instance contrary to the light which he hath given thee.

John Wesley, 1703-1791, England

But woe unto those weak and timid souls who are divided between God and their world! They want and they do not want. They are torn by passion and remorse at the same time. They fear the judgments of God and those of others. They have a horror of evil and a shame of good. They have the pains of virtue without tasting its sweet consolations. O, how wretched they are! Ah, if they had a little courage to despise the empty talk, the cold mockings, and the rash criticism of others, what peace they would enjoy in the bosom of God!

How dangerous it is for our salvation, how unworthy of God and of ourselves, how pernicious even for the peace of our hearts, to want always to stay where we are! Our whole life was only given us to advance us by great strides toward our heavenly country. The world escapes like a delusive shadow. Eternity already advances to receive us. Why do we delay to advance while the light of the Father of mercies shines for us? Let us hasten to reach the kingdom of God.

François Fénelon, 1651-1715, France

The moment I realized that God existed, I knew I could not do otherwise than to live for Him alone.

Charles de Foucauld, 1858-1916, France

Ho, everyone who thirsts,
  come to the waters;
and you that have no money,
  come, buy and eat!
Come, buy wine and milk
  without money and without price.
Why do you spend your money
    for that which is not bread,
  and your labor for that
    which does not satisfy?
Listen carefully to me, and eat
    what is good,
  and delight yourselves in rich food.
Incline your ear, and come to me;
  listen, so that you may live.

Isaiah 55:1-3

Listen! I am standing at the door, knocking; if you hear my voice
and open the door, I will come in to you and eat with you, and
you with me.

Revelation 3:20

Be free, therefore, and free yourself from every kind of destruc-
tive slavery. For unless you become free, you cannot be a worker
for Christ; for that kingdom in the heavenly Jerusalem which is free
does not accept children of slavery. The children of a free mother
are themselves free, (see Romans 8:15) and are not enslaved to the
world in anything (see Galatians 4:23).

John the Solitary, fifth century, West Syria

"Ask, and it will be given you; search, and you will find; knock,
and the door will be opened for you. For everyone who asks
receives, and everyone who searches finds, and for everyone who
knocks, the door will be opened. Is there anyone among you who,
if your child asks for bread, will give a stone? Or if the child asks
for a fish, will give a snake? If you then, who are evil, know how
to give good gifts to your children, how much more will your
Father in heaven give good things to those who ask him!"

Matthew 7:7-11

Gracious Voices

The inward stirring and touching of God makes us hungry and
yearning; for the Spirit of God haunts our spirit; and the more he
touches it, the greater our hunger and craving.

Jan van Ruysbroeck, 1293?-1381, Holland

RESPONSE TO GOD'S CALL

As Jesus passed along the Sea of Galilee, he saw Simon and his brother Andrew casting a net into the sea—for they were fishermen. And Jesus said to them, "Follow me and I will make you fish for people." And immediately they left their nets and followed him.

Mark 1:16-18

I am the light of the world. Whoever follows me will never walk in darkness but will have the light of life.

John 8:12

Receive the mark of the cross on your forehead,
as a sign of the way you are to follow
and as a sign that Christ is with you in strength and love.
May the power of the Holy Spirit enable you to know and follow him.
Amen.

A Service for the Welcoming of Hearers, *Come to the Waters*

Lord, I shall openly sign all my limbs
with the sign of your Cross,
as you have said, do you, Lord,
mark me in a hidden way
with the truth of your Cross.

Joseph the Visionary, eighth century, East Syria

An old man was asked, "What is the straight and narrow way?" He replied, "The straight way is this, to do violence to one's thoughts and to cut off one's own will. That is what this means: 'Behold we have left all and followed thee'." (Mark 10:28)

a saying of the Desert Fathers, fourth-fifth centuries, Syria/Palestine/Egypt

Then he said to them all "If any want to become my followers, let them deny themselves and take up their cross daily and follow me. For those who want to save their life will lose it, and those who lose their life for my sake will save jt."

Luke 9:23-24

Since, by assenting to what belongs to faith, man is raised above his nature, this must needs come to him from some supernatural principle moving him inwardly, and this is God. Therefore faith, as regards the assent which is the chief act of faith, is from God moving inwardly by grace.

Thomas Aquinas, 1227?-1274?, Italy

Now faith is the assurance of things hoped for, the conviction of things not seen.

Hebrews 11:1

Faith is a living and unshakable confidence, a belief in the grace of God so assured that one could die a thousand deaths for its sake. This kind of confidence in God's grace, this sort of knowledge of it, makes us joyful, high-spirited, and eager in our relations with God and with all people. That is what the Holy Spirit effects through faith. Hence, the person of faith, without being driven willingly and gladly seeks to do good to everyone, serve everyone, suffer all kinds of hardships, for the sake of the love and glory of the God who has shown such grace. It is impossible, indeed, to separate works from faith, just as it is impossible to separate heat and light from fire.

Martin Luther, 1483-1546, Germany

A scribe then approached and said, "Teacher, I will follow you wherever you go." And Jesus said to him, "Foxes have holes, and birds of the air have nests; but the Son of Man has nowhere to lay his head." Another of his disciples said to him, "Lord, first let me go and bury my father." But Jesus said to him, "Follow me, and let the dead bury their dead."

Matthew 8:19-22

Faith means just that blessed unrest, deep and strong, which so urges the believer onward that he cannot settle at ease in the world and anyone who was quite at ease would cease to be a believer.

Søren Kierkegaard, 1813-1855, Denmark

Simple faith is necessary in seeking God. In outward things, light helps to prevent one from falling; but in the things of God just the opposite is true: it is better for the soul not to see if it is to be more secure.

John of the Cross, 1542-1591, Spain

Wednesday, August 10, 1774. I was very low, but met my class, and preached in the evening. There appeared to be but little depth of religion in the class. It is a great folly to take people into society before they know what they are about. What some people take for religion and spiritual life, is nothing but the power of the natural passions. It is true, real religion cannot exist without peace, and love, and joy. But then, real religion is real holiness. And all sensations without a strong disposition for holiness, are but delusive.

Francis Asbury, 1745-1816, United States

Gracious Voices

Introduction to Making a Choice of a State or Way of Life

In making a choice or in coming to a decision, only one thing is really important—to seek and to find what God calls me to at this time of my life. I know that his call remains faithful; he has created me for himself and my salvation is found in that love. All my choices, then, must be consistent with this given direction of my life.

It becomes obvious how easy it is for me to forget such a simple truth as the end and goal of my whole existence when I consider the manner in which choices are often made. Many people, for example, choose marriage, which is a means, and only secondarily consider the service of God our Lord in marriage, though to do the will of God is each person's end and goal. Many people first choose to make a lot of money or to be successful, and only afterwards to be able to serve God by it. And so too in their striving for power, popularity, and so on. All of these people exhibit an attitude of putting God into second place, and they want God to come into their lives only after their own disordered attachment. In other words, they mix up the order of an end and a means to that end. What they ought to seek first and above all else, they often put last.

It is good, then, for me to recall that my whole aim in life should be to seek to serve God in whatever way his call may come to me. Keeping clearly before me my desire to serve God our Lord, I can begin to search out the means of marrying or not marrying, a life of business involvement or a life of simple frugality, and the like, for these are all means to accomplishing the end. I will choose to use or not to use such means only through the inspiration and movement of God's grace leading me on in his service and to my own salvation.

Ignatius of Loyola, 1491?-1556, Spain

Late have I loved you, O Beauty so ancient and so new; late have I loved you! For behold you were within me, and I outside; and I sought you outside and in my unloveliness fell upon those lovely things that you have made. You were with me and I was not with you. I was kept from you by those things, yet had they not been in you, you would not have been at all. You called and cried to me to break open my deafness: and you sent forth your beams and shone upon me and chased away my blindness: You breathed fragrance upon me, and I drew in my breath and do now pant for you: I tasted you, and now hunger and thirst for you: You touched me, and I have burned for your peace.

Augustine, 354-430, North Africa

Faith is different from proof; the latter is human, the former is a gift of God.

Blaise Pascal, 1623-1662, France

THE COMMUNITY OF FAITH WELCOMES YOU

Then the word of the LORD came to him (Elijah), saying, "Go now to Zarephath, which belongs to Sidon, and live there; for I have commanded a widow there to feed you." So he set out and went to Zarephath. When he came to the gate of the town, a widow was there gathering sticks; he called to her and said, "Bring me a little water in a vessel, so that I may drink." As she was going to bring it, he called to her and said, "Bring me a morsel of bread in your hand." But she said, "As the LORD your God lives, I have nothing baked, only a handful of meal in a jar, and a little oil in a jug; I am now gathering a couple of sticks, so that I may go home and prepare it for myself and my son, that we may eat it, and die." Elijah said to her, "Do not be afraid; go and do as you have said; but first make me a little cake of it and bring it to me, and afterwards make something for yourself and your son. For thus says the LORD the God of Israel: The jar of meal will not be emptied and the jug of oil will not fail until the day that the LORD sends rain on the earth." She went and did as Elijah said, so that she as well as he and her household ate for many days. The jar of meal was not emptied, neither did the jug of oil fail, according to the word of the LORD that he spoke by Elijah.

1 Kings 17:8-16

At first the word "hospitality" might evoke the image of soft sweet kindness, tea parties, bland conversations, and a general atmosphere of coziness. Probably this has its good reasons since in our culture the concept of hospitality has lost much of its power and is often used in circles where we are more prone to expect a watered down piety than a serious search for an authentic Christian spirituality. But still, if there is any concept worth restoring to its original depth and evocative potential, it is the concept of hospitality. It is one of the richest biblical terms that can deepen and broaden our insight into our relationships with our fellow human beings. . . .

When hostility is converted into hospitality then fearful strangers can become guests revealing to their hosts the promise they are carrying with them. Then, in fact, the distinction between host and guest proves to be artificial and evaporates in the recognition of the new-found unity.

Henri J. M. Nouwen, 1932-1996, United States

Where charity and love prevail, there God is ever found;
brought here together by Christ's love, by love are we thus bound.

Forgive we now each other's faults as we our faults confess;
and let us love each other well in Christian holiness.

Omer Westendorf, United States

Love bade me welcome; yet my soul drew back,
    Guilty of dust and sin.
But quick-eyed Love, observing me grow slack
    From my first entrance in,
Drew nearer to me, sweetly questioning
    If I lacked anything.

"A guest," I answered, "worthy to be here."
    Love said, "You shall be he."
"I, the unkind, ungrateful? Ah, my dear,
    I cannot look on Thee."
Love took my hand, and smiling, did reply,
    "Who made the eyes but I?"

"Truth, Lord, but I have marred them; let my shame
    Go where it doth deserve."
"And know you not," says Love, "who bore the
        blame?"
    "My dear, then I will serve."
"You must sit down," says Love, "and taste my meat."
    So I did sit and eat.

George Herbert, 1593-1633, England

Do everything in common:
Unite in one prayer, one petition,
one mind, one hope,
in love and faultless joy.
All this is Jesus Christ,
and there is nothing better than he.
So make haste, all of you,
to come together as to one temple of God,
around one altar,
around the one Jesus Christ,
who came forth from the one Father,
while still remaining one with him,
and has returned to unity with him.

Ignatius of Antioch, late first/early second century

Christianity is more than a matter of a new understanding.
Christianity is an invitation to be part of an alien people who make
a difference because they see something that cannot otherwise be
seen without Christ. Right living is more the challenge than right
thinking. The challenge is not the intellectual one but the political
one—the creation of a new people who have aligned themselves
with the seismic shift that has occurred in the world since Christ.

Stanley Hauerwas and William Willimon, United States

Console
yourself:
You would
not be
seeking
me if you
had not
already
found me.

Blaise Pascal,
1623-1662,
France

It is therefore expected of all who continue [in the Methodist societies] that they should continue to evidence their desire of salvation,

First: By doing no harm, by avoiding evil of every kind, especially that which is most generally practiced, such as:

The taking of the name of God in vain.

The profaning of the day of the Lord, either by doing ordinary work therein or by buying or selling.

Drunkenness: buying or selling spirituous liquors, or drinking them, unless in cases of extreme necessity. . . .

Fighting, quarreling, brawling, brother going to law with brother; returning evil for evil, or railing for railing; the using of many words in buying or selling. . . .

Doing to others as we would not they should do unto us. . . .

The taking such diversions as cannot be used in the name of the Lord Jesus. . . .

It is expected of all who continue in these societies that they should continue to evidence their desire of salvation . . .

By doing good; by being in every kind merciful after their power; as they have opportunity, doing good of every possible sort, and, as far as possible, to all . . .

It is expected of all who desire to continue in these societies that they should continue to evidence their desire of salvation. . .

By attending upon all the ordinances of God; such are:

The public worship of God.

The ministry of the Word, either read or expounded.

The Supper of the Lord.

Family and private prayer.

Searching the Scriptures.

Fasting or abstinence.

The General Rules of the Methodist Societies, 1739

You have come from afar
and waited long and are wearied:
Let us sit side by side
sharing the same bread drawn from the same source
to quiet the same hunger that makes us weak.
Then standing together
let us share the same spirit, the same thoughts
that once again draw us together in friendship and unity and peace.

Prieres d'Ozawamick, Native Canadian

Gracious Voices

Christianity is not, and never has been, a solitary faith. When one asks, "Does one need to go to church to be a Christian?" he is putting the question the wrong way around. One might better say, "If one is a Christian, will he not wish to unite with other Christians in public worship?"

Georgia Harkness, 1891-1974, United States

Many people seek fellowship because they are afraid to be alone. Because they cannot stand loneliness, they are driven to seek the company of other people. There are Christians, too, who cannot endure being alone, who have had some bad experiences with themselves, who hope they will gain some help in association with others. They are generally disappointed. Then they blame the fellowship for what is really their own fault. The Christian community is not a spiritual sanatorium. The person who comes into a fellowship because he is running away from himself is misusing it for the sake of diversion, no matter how spiritual this diversion may appear. He is really not seeking community at all, but only distraction which will allow him to forget his loneliness for a brief time, the very alienation that creates the deadly isolation of man. The disintegration of communication and all genuine experience, and finally resignation and spiritual death are the result of such attempts to find a cure. . . .

Let him who cannot be alone beware of community. He will only do harm to himself and to the community. Alone you stood before God when he called you; alone you had to answer that call; alone you had to struggle and pray; and alone you will die and give an account to God. You cannot escape from yourself; for God has singled you out. If you refuse to be alone you are rejecting Christ's call to you, and you can have no part in the community of those who are called. . . .

But the reverse is also true: Let him who is not in community beware of being alone. Into the community you were called, the call was not meant for you alone; in the community of the called you bear your cross, you struggle, you pray. You are not alone, even in death, and on the Last Day you will be only one member of the great congregation of Jesus Christ. If you scorn the fellowship of the brethren, you reject the call of Jesus Christ, and thus your solitude can only be hurtful to you. . . .

We recognize, then, that only as we are within the fellowship can we be alone, and only he that is alone can live in the fellowship. Only in the fellowship do we learn to be rightly alone and only in aloneness do we learn to live rightly in the fellowship. It is not as though the one preceded the other; both begin at the same time, namely, with the call of Jesus Christ.

Dietrich Bonhoeffer, 1906-1945, Germany

Nothing is so con-ducive to unity as rejoicing about the same things and holding to the same purpose.

Dorotheus of Gaza, sixth century

BECOMING A DISCIPLE

As soon as April pierces to the root
The drought of March, and bathes each bud and shoot
Through every vein of sap with gentle showers
From whose engendering liquor spring the flowers;
When zephyrs have breathed softly all about
Inspiring every wood and field to sprout,
And in the zodiac the youthful sun
His journey halfway through the Ram has run;
When little birds are busy with their song
Who sleep with open eyes the whole night long
Life stirs their hearts and tingles in them so,
Then off as pilgrims people long to go.

Geoffrey Chaucer, fourteenth century, England

Christian life originated in God-walk, on the road, in the market-place, by the seaside, and outside a city wall in a criminal's death on a cross. "Disciple" is a word we use for someone who joins in the walk. Discipleship is the first and decisive word for God-walk in Christianity. It covers a way of life. It does not say: what you do is what counts. What counts is where your head is and where your heart is. "Where your treasure is, there is your heart also" (Matthew 6:21).

In other words, God-walk means willingness to immerse one-self in life as a whole and to stand where Jesus stands in all walks of life, especially with those whom society tunes out: the invisible women and men, also the injured creation. That is why the eucharist is so central. Only here do we touch—as it were, bodi-ly—the real presence of God in history in terms of Christian community.

So it is not activity in general that is called for when we reflect on our social location. It is first of all participation in the justice mission of Jesus. It is eucharistic action. It is immersion in conflict, with class struggle at the cutting edge. It is immersion in conflict because Jesus is still caught up in conflict. Jesus' life has not come to an end as yet. It is still going on.

Frederick Herzog, 1925-1995, United States

God be in your head, and in your understanding.
God be in your eyes, and in your looking.
God be in your mouth, and in your speaking.
God be in your heart, and in your thinking.
God be at your end, and at your departing.

Sarum Liturgy, thirteenth century, England

Gracious Voices

We have this grace, not only from Christ, but in him. For our perfection is not like that of a tree, which flourishes by the sap derived from its own root, but, as was said before, like that of a branch which, united to the vine, bears fruit; but severed from it, is dried up and withered.

John Wesley, 1703-1791, England

An old man was asked, "How can I find God?" He said, "In fasting, in watching, in labors, in devotion, and, above all, in discernment. I tell you, many have injured their bodies without discernment and have gone away from us having achieved nothing. Our mouths smell bad through fasting, we know the Scriptures by heart, we recite all the Psalms of David, but we have not that which God seeks: charity and humility."

a saying of the Desert Fathers, fourth-fifth centuries, Syria/Palestine/Egypt

One thing I have never understood is how Christians have gotten the image of being dull, uninteresting, and dedicated to lives devoid of all humor, excitement, and adventure.

The fun of being a Christian—and that is what it is—is awakening each morning with the possibility of a new step, a new enlightenment, a fresh facet of Christ burning in on us. People and things quickly become pretty predictable, but Christ—never!

I've never fully empathized with those who lean their entire faith on a few selected verses from the Bible, or on carefully chosen, regularly meeting church groups and activities. Even in the regular church service, with the regular form and the regular content, one can't stifle the inventiveness of God. From out of static, Sunday-worn monotony leaps a phrase from a song, a line from the Scripture, and the world-beat skips for us.

Often people talk about relying on Christ for the deeps of faith, hope, and peace. I do too. But the most enchanting thing that I rely upon is his ability to see through the mist of my insufficiency and awkwardness, spot the moment that is right, and spring a new lock that flings open the door to a fresh vista.

Sometimes it comes when I'm alone. Sometimes when I'm listening to another. Sometimes at work. I've even waked out of a sound sleep from a tap of Christ. Sometimes I see it; other times I hear it, or feel it. Always it makes me smile.

It must be very dull not to be a searching Christian, and never know the surprise of Christ.

Lois Cheney, United States

The daring ambition of aspiring to great sanctity has never left me. I don't rely on my own merits, because I haven't any; I put all my confidence in him who is virtue, who is holiness itself.

Thérèse de Lisieux, 1873-1897, France

Q: What is Christian Perfection?

A: The loving God with all our heart, mind, soul, and strength. This implies that no wrong temper, none contrary to love, remains in the soul; and that all the thoughts, words, and actions are governed by pure love.

John Wesley, 1703–1791, England

This is true perfection: not to avoid a wicked life because like slaves we servilely fear punishment, nor to do good because we hope for rewards, as if cashing in on the virtuous life by some business-like arrangement. On the contrary, disregarding all those things for which we hope and which have been reserved by promise, we regard falling from God's friendship as the only thing dreadful and we consider becoming God's friend the only thing worthy of honor and desire. This, as I have said, is the perfection of life.

Gregory of Nyssa, 331?–394, Asia Minor

Jesus had come to redeem the world—to teach us that love of his Father. How strange that he should spend thirty years just doing nothing, wasting his time! Not giving a chance to his personality or to his gifts, for we know that at the age of twelve he silenced the learned priests of the temple, who knew so much and so well. But when his parents found him, he went down to Nazareth and was subject to them. For thirty years we hear no more of him—so that the people were astonished when he came in public to preach, he a carpenter's son, doing just the humble work in a carpenter's shop—for thirty years!

Knowledge of God gives love and knowledge of self gives humility. Humility is nothing but truth. What have we got that we have not received? asks St. Paul. If I have received everything, what good have I of my own? If we are convinced of this we will never raise our head in pride. If you are humble nothing will touch you, neither praise nor disgrace, because you know what you are. If you are blamed you will not be discouraged. If they call you a saint you will not put yourself on a pedestal.

Self-knowledge puts us on our knees.

Mother Teresa of Calcutta, India

I want Jesus to walk with me.
I want Jesus to walk with me.
All along my pilgrim journey,
Lord, I want Jesus to walk with me.

African–American Spiritual

A God-seeker is a person on a journey. When the thirst has been awakened, we are no longer persons wandering aimlessly about, but rather persons who have begun to discern the bare outlines of a path. We become more than wanderers. We are people seeking for those signs that will point us in the direction that will allow our journey to unfold. For those whose thirst has led them into an encounter with Jesus of Nazareth, the signs that mark the way are grounded in an ancient and consistent tradition.

The Christian journey is indissolubly linked with a person. It is not a journey that we take alone. "Since Jesus was delivered to you as Christ and Lord," wrote St. Paul to that fledgling community of Christians gathered in the city of Colossae, "live your lives in union with him. Be rooted in him, be built in him, be consolidated in the faith you were taught; let your hearts overflow with thankfulness" (Colossians 2:6-8).

Paul's words are not so much an injunction as they are a description of a relationship—a relationship already initiated by God's act. At the very moment we discover within ourselves the urge to respond to those deep yearnings that are so hard to put into words, we discover to our surprise that we have not chosen Him, but rather He has chosen us. In this recognition the journey of faith begins.

The Scriptures are full of stories about new beginnings. "The time has come," Jesus told the crowds as he made his way through Galilee. "The kingdom of God is upon you; repent and believe the Gospel" (Mark 1:15). This is where it all starts. We come to that point in our lives when we are ready to make a turn—to put behind us all those things that have bent our lives out of shape—and to enter into a new kind of relationship based on the belief that Jesus Christ is as present to us today as he was in the first century.

The Christian faith is a story of new beginnings. It is a story of repentance and forgiveness, of life emerging out of the experience of death. It is a journey which begins with the recognition that there is more to life than meets the eye—that without the healing and sustaining power of God our lives are incomplete. It is a journey which begins with the incredible fact of our unconditional acceptance by God. There is nothing we can do to earn or prove our worth. Our worth has been affirmed once and for all by the offering of Jesus Christ on our behalf. The Christian journey begins when, as forgiven and affirmed people, we ever so tentatively risk letting our lives be shaped and empowered by the Person of Jesus Christ. As the Gospel proclaims, because He lives, we live also with new possibility and purpose. Instead of being "takers," we become "givers," members of a community struggling to live in the world in a new way.

James C. Fenhagen, United States

Not happiness first and holiness if possible, but holiness first and bliss as a consequence.

W. E. Sangster, 1900-1960, England

Our perfection doth certainly consist in knowing God and ourselves.

Angela of Foligno, 1248-1309, Italy

JOINING IN PRAYER AND WORSHIP

Worship, in all its grades and kinds, is the response of the creature to the Eternal: nor need we limit this definition to the human sphere. There is a sense in which we may think of the whole life of the Universe, seen and unseen, conscious and unconscious, as an act of worship, glorifying its Origin, Sustainer, and End.

Evelyn Underhill, 1875-1941, England

Grant, O Lord,
    that what has been said with our lips we
        may believe in our hearts,
    and that what we believe in our hearts
        we may practice in our lives;
        through Jesus Christ our Lord. Amen.

John Hunter, 1848-1917, Scotland

My prayers must meet a brazen heaven
and fail or scatter all away.
Unclean and seeming unforgiven
My prayers I scarcely call to pray.
I cannot buoy my heart above;
Above it cannot entrance win.
I reckon precedents of love,
But feel the long success of sin.

My heaven is brass and iron my earth:
Yea iron is mingled with my clay
So harden'd is it in this dearth
Which praying fails to do away.
Nor tears, nor tears this clay uncouth
Could mould, if any tears there were.
A warfare of my lips in truth,
Battling with God, is now my prayer.

Gerard Manley Hopkins, 1844-1889, England

From hence it clearly and certainly appears, that great part of true religion consists in the affections. For love is not only one of the affections, but it is the first and chief of the affections, and the fountain of all the affections. From love arises hatred of those things which are contrary to what we love, or which oppose and thwart us in those things that we delight in: and from the various exercises of love and hatred, according to the circumstances of the objects of these affections, as present or absent, certain or uncertain, probable or improbable, arise all those other affections of desire, hope, fear, joy, grief, gratitude, anger, etc. From a vigorous, affectionate, and fervent love to God, will necessarily arise other religious affections; hence will arise an intense hatred and abhorrence of sin, fear of

Gracious Voices

sin, and a dread of God's displeasure, gratitude to God for his goodness, complacence and joy in God, when God is graciously and sensibly present, and grief when he is absent, and a joyful hope when a future enjoyment of God is expected, and fervent zeal for the glory of God. And in like manner, from a fervent love to men, will arise all other virtuous affections towards men.

Jonathan Edwards, 1703-1758, New England

The time of business does not with me differ from the time of prayer, and in the noise and clatter of my kitchen, while several persons are at the same time calling for different things, I possess God in as great tranquillity as if I were upon my knees at the blessed sacrament.

Brother Lawrence, 1611-1691, France

O God, drive me in like a nail into mahogany, a nail which cannot be pulled out.

prayer from Nigeria

LIVING WITH THE SCRIPTURES

Understanding is the reward of faith. Therefore seek not to understand that you may believe, but believe that you may understand.

Augustine, 354-430, North Africa

Come, divine Interpreter,
bring me eyes thy book to read,
ears the mystic words to hear,
words which did from thee proceed,
words that endless bliss impart,
kept in an obedient heart.

All who read, or hear, are blessed,
if thy plain commands we do;
of thy kingdom here possessed,
thee we shall in glory view
when thou comest on earth to abide,
reign triumphant at thy side.

Charles Wesley, 1707-1788, England

From the cowardice that dares not face new truth,
from the laziness that is contented with half-truth,
from the arrogance that thinks it knows all truth,
Good Lord, deliver me. Amen.

prayer from Kenya

Toil at reading the Scriptures more than anything else: for in prayer the mind frequently wanders, but in reading even a wandering mind is recollected.

John the Solitary, fifth century, West Syria

United Methodists share with other Christians the conviction that Scripture is the primary source and criterion for Christian doctrine. Through Scripture the living Christ meets us in the experience of redeeming grace. We are convinced that Jesus Christ is the living Word of God in our midst whom we trust in life and death.

The biblical authors, illumined by the Holy Spirit, bear witness that in Christ the world is reconciled to God. The Bible bears authentic testimony to God's self-disclosure in the life, death, and resurrection of Jesus Christ as well as in God's work of creation, in the pilgrimage of Israel, and in the Holy Spirit's ongoing activity in human history.

As we open our minds and hearts to the Word of God through the words of human beings inspired by the Holy Spirit, faith is born and nourished, our understanding is deepened, and the possibilities for transforming the world become apparent to us.

We properly read Scripture within the believing community, informed by the tradition of that community. We interpret individual texts in light of their place in the Bible as a whole.

The Book of Discipline of The United Methodist Church, 1992

Blessed Lord, who caused all holy Scriptures to be written for our learning: Grant us so to hear them, read, mark, learn, and inwardly digest them, that we may embrace and ever hold fast the blessed hope of everlasting life, which you have given us in our Savior Jesus Christ; who lives and reigns with you and the Holy Spirit, one God, for ever and ever. Amen.

The Book of Common Prayer

"Praying the Scripture" is a unique way of dealing with the Scripture; it involves both reading and prayer. Turn to the Scripture; choose some passage that is simple and fairly practical. Next, come to the Lord. Come quietly and humbly. There, before him, read a small portion of the passage of Scripture you have opened to.

Be careful as you read. Take in fully, gently, and carefully what you are reading. Taste it and digest it as you read. In the past it may have been your habit, while reading, to move very quickly from one verse of Scripture to another until you have read the whole passage. Perhaps you were seeking to find the main point of the passage.

But in coming to the Lord by means of "praying the Scripture," you do not read quickly; you read very slowly. You do not move from one passage to another, not until you have *sensed* the very heart of what you have read. You may then want to take that portion of Scripture that has touched you and turn to it in prayer.

After you have sensed something of the passage, and after you know that the essence of that portion has been extracted and all the deeper sense of it is gone, then, very slowly, gently, and in a calmer manner begin to read the next portion of that passage. You will be surprised to find that when your time with the Lord has ended, you will have read very little, probably no more than half a page.

"Praying the Scripture" is not judged by *how much* you read but by the *way* you read. If you read quickly, it will benefit you little. You will be like a bee that merely skims the surface of a flower. Instead, in this new way of reading with prayer, you become as the bee who penetrates into the depths of the flower. You plunge deeply within to remove its deepest nectar.

Of course, there is a kind of reading the Scripture for scholarship and for study—but not here. That studious kind of reading will not help you when it comes to matters that are divine! To receive any deep, inward profit from the Scripture you must read as I have described. Plunge into the very depths of the words you read until revelation, like a sweet aroma, breaks out upon you. I am quite sure that if you will follow this course, little by little you will come to experience a very rich prayer that flows from your inward being.

Madame Guyon, 1648-1717, France

If we pray
we will
believe
If we
believe
we will love
If we love
we will
serve.

Mother Teresa
of Calcutta,
India

BECOMING A SERVANT

Some may, perhaps, say, "Well, I have refrained from debauchery, folly and idleness; I have earned my honest penny, and kept it, and laid up a comfortable provision for my family." Be it so; this is laudable and praiseworthy, and it were to be wished that many more in this country would do so much. But may not such a one be asked, have you been charitable withal? Have you been as industrious in laying up treasures in heaven, as you have been in hoarding up the perishable riches of this world? Have you stretched out your hand, as you had opportunity, beyond the circle of your own house and family? Have your poorer neighbors cause to bless you for your kind and charitable assistance? Have you dedicated any portion of your labors to God, who blessed them, by doing good to any besides your own? Has the stranger, the widow or the fatherless ever tasted of your bounty? If you have never done things of this kind, but have hitherto slighted, overlooked or put off occasions of this sort, your talent is as yet hid in a napkin, it lies yet buried in the ground, huddled up within yourself. And consider further, that the real poor and needy are Christ's representatives.

Richard Allen, 1760-1831, United States

A Christian is a perfectly free lord of all, subject to none.
A Christian is a perfectly dutiful servant of all, subject to all.

Martin Luther, 1483-1547, Germany

A man possessed by the devil, who was foaming terribly at the mouth, struck a hermit-monk on the cheek. The old man turned and offered him the other. Then the devil, unable to bear the burning of humility, disappeared immediately.

a saying of the Desert Fathers, fourth-fifth centuries, Syria/Palestine/Egypt

Serve your God with patience and passion.
Be deliberate in enacting your faith.
Be steadfast in celebrating the Spirit's power.
And may peace be your way in the world. Amen.

Glen E. Rainsley, United States

It was said of a brother that having made some baskets he was putting on the handles when he heard his neighbor saying, "What can I do? Market day is near and I have no handles to put on my baskets." Then he took the handles off his own baskets and brought them to the brother, saying, "Here are these handles which I have over; take them and put them on your baskets." So he caused his brother's work to succeed by neglecting his own.

a saying of the Desert Fathers, Fourth-Fifth centuries, Syria/Palestine/Egypt

Do you want to honor Christ's body? Then do not scorn him in his nakedness, nor honor him here in the church with silken garments while neglecting him outside where he is cold and naked.

John Chrysostom, 345?-407, West Syria

When we only seek eminence and position, how few avenues are open! When we seek service, how many—all with wide gates, and loud calls, and pleading invitations, to come where work, and room, and reward await all!

Isabella Thoburn, 1840-1901

Then the king will say to those at his right hand, "Come, you that are blessed by my Father, inherit the kingdom prepared for you from the foundation of the world; for I was hungry and you gave me food, I was thirsty and you gave me something to drink, I was a stranger and you welcomed me, I was naked and you gave me clothing, I was sick and you took care of me, I was in prison and you visited me." Then the righteous will answer him, 'Lord, when was it that we saw you hungry and gave you food, or thirsty and gave you something to drink? And when was it that we saw you a stranger and welcomed you, or naked and gave you clothing? And when was it that we saw you sick or in prison and visited you?' And the king will answer them, "Truly I tell you, just as you did it to one of the least of these who are members of my family, you did it to me. "

Matthew 25:31-40

Gracious Voices

THE APOSTLES' CREED

I believe in God, the Father Almighty,
   creator of heaven and earth.

I believe in Jesus Christ, his only Son, our Lord,
   who was conceived by the Holy Spirit,
   born of the Virgin Mary,
   suffered under Pontius Pilate,
   was crucified, died, and was buried;
   he descended to the dead.
   On the third day he rose again;
   he ascended into heaven,
   is seated at the right hand of the Father,
   and will come again to judge the living and the dead.

I believe in the Holy Spirit,
   the holy catholic church,
   the communion of saints,
   the forgiveness of sins,
   the resurrection of the body
   and the life everlasting. Amen.

I believe in God, the Father Almighty, creator of heaven and earth.

Eternal Father:
When nothing existed but chaos,
   you swept across the dark waters
   and brought forth light.

Thanksgiving over the Water, Baptismal Covenant

Describe [God] as you will: good, fair Lord, sweet, merciful,
righteous, wise, all-knowing, strong one, almighty; as knowledge,
wisdom, might, strength, love, or charity, and you will find them
all hidden and contained in this little word *is*.

Anonymous, *The Book of Privy Counseling*, fourteenth century, England

Like the sun that is far away and yet close at hand to warm us,
   so God's Spirit is ever present and around us.
Come Creator into our lives.
We live and move and have our very being in you.
Open now the windows of our souls.

United Methodist Clergywomen's Consultation

Calling to Baptism:
Professing and Praying with the Church

CALLING TO
BAPTISM:

Professing
and Praying
with the
Church

The stories about the patriarchs, which are many, are human stories of belief and unbelief, strength and weakness, vision of faith and shortsightedness, humility and arrogance, reconciliation and conflict. They are absolutely fascinating stories pointing to the living reality of the God who rules over the history of man. All these stories are precisely meant to be there when God quoted these three names. Not just the inspiring parts of their life stories, but the whole of their lives are quoted in the solemn context of God's self-introduction.

The holy God introduces himself by quoting these three human names as though they were the only proper way to introduce himself. "This is my name for ever and thus I am to be remembered throughout all generations!" This is the Gospel. Our human names are quoted in God's self-introduction, we ourselves are introduced in the most fundamental and profound way, the depth of which perhaps none of us will ever be able to understand.

Kosuke Koyama, Japan

Suppose someone asked me, when I see a man in a blue uniform going down the street leaving little paper packets at each house, why I suppose that they contain letters? I should reply, "Because whenever he leaves a similar little packet for me I find it does contain a letter." And if he then objected, "But you've never seen all these letters which you think the other people are getting," I should say, "Of course not, and I shouldn't expect to, because they're not addressed to me I'm explaining the packets I'm not allowed to open by the ones I'm allowed to open." It is the same about this question. The only packet I'm allowed to open is Man. When I do, especially when I open that particular man called Myself, I find that I do not exist on my own, that I am under a law; that somebody or something wants me to behave in a certain way. I do not, of course, think that if I could get inside a stone or a tree I should find exactly the same thing, just as I do not think all the other people in the street get the same letters as I do. I should expect, for instance, to find that the stone had to obey the law of gravity—that whereas the sender of the letters merely tells me to obey the laws of my human nature, He compels the stone to obey the laws of its stony nature. But I should expect to find that there was, so to speak, a sender of letters in both cases, a Power behind the facts, a Director, a Guide.

C. S. Lewis, 1898-1963, England

Maker, in whom we live, in whom we are and move,
the glory, power, and praise receive for thy creating love.
Let all the angel throng give thanks to God on high,
while earth repeats the joyful song and echoes to the sky.

Charles Wesley, 1707-1788, England

For the first year I commonly employed myself during the time set apart for devotion with the thought of death, judgment, heaven, hell, and my sins. Thus I continued some years, applying my mind carefully the rest of the day, even in the midst of my business, *to the presence of God,* whom I considered always as with me, often as *in* me.

At length I came insensibly to do the same thing during my set time of prayer, which caused in me great delight and consolation. This practice produced in me so high an esteem for God that *faith* alone was capable to satisfy me in that point.

Brother Lawrence, 1611-1691, France

To call God "Father," then, is not to claim something *about* God but to claim something *from* God. It is to claim God's promises, to call God to be near even though he seems far away.

Theodore Jennings, United States

God of us all, your love never ends.
When all else fails, you are still God.

Commendation Prayers, Service of Death and Resurrection

Then the LORD answered Job out of the whirlwind:
"Who is this that darkens counsel by words without knowledge?
Gird up your loins like a man,
I will question you, and you shall declare to me.
"Where were you when I laid the foundation of the earth?
Tell me, if you have understanding.
Who determined its measurements—surely you know!
Or who stretched the line upon it?
On what were its bases sunk,
or who laid its cornerstone
when the morning stars sang together
and all the heavenly beings shouted for joy?"

Job 38:1-7

God, who stretched the spangled heavens, infinite in time and place,
flung the suns in burning radiance through the silent fields of space,
we your children, in your likeness, share inventive powers with you.
Great Creator, still creating, show us what we yet may do.

Catherine Cameron, Canada

If you contemplate God with the eyes of faith, you will see Him just as He is, and, in a certain manner, face to face.

attributed to John Eudes, 1601-1680, France

Though we cannot know God, we can love God: by love God may be touched and embraced, never by thought.

Anonymous, *The Cloud of Unknowing,* fourteenth century, England

CALLING TO
BAPTISM:

Professing
and Praying
with the
Church

God is creating all things *now*. When we look at an oak tree we can glimpse this. The tree is there because God is creating it at this moment. If he were not doing so, it would not be there.

It is an oak, and not a beech or a chestnut, because that is the way God is creating it. It is alive and growing, forming shoots in spring and acorns in autumn, because God is creating it, loving it, and giving it life. . . .

God is also creating (and therefore loving) all human beings, even those whom we do not like and those who (like ourselves) often do what God does not like. Whenever we meet another person, whether in friendship or in a difficult interview, God is creating both of us, helping us to work out his will.

Dom Robert Petitpierre, Englandl

Wherever you cast your eyes, there is no spot in the universe wherein you cannot discern at least some sparks of his glory. You cannot in one glance survey the most vast and beautiful system of the universe, in its wide expanse, without being completely overwhelmed by the boundless force of its brightness. The reason why the author of The Letter to the Hebrews elegantly calls the universe the appearance of things invisible (Hebrews 11:3) is that this skillful ordering of the universe is for us a sort of mirror in which we can contemplate God, who is otherwise invisible.

John Calvin, 1509-1564, France

The transcendence of God passes all our understanding. Yet it does not pass our understanding that only a God of just such transcendent greatness, so far removed from our own limitations, could be always so near, so aware of our innermost thoughts, and so sensitive of our every need as faith affirms God to be in his immanence.

L. Harold DeWolf, United States

The almighty, the all-wise God sees and knows, from everlasting to everlasting, all that is, that was, that is to come, through one eternal *now*.

John Wesley , 1703-1791, England

I sing the almighty power of God, that made the mountains rise,
that spread the flowing seas abroad and built the lofty skies.
I sing the wisdom that ordained the sun to rule the day;
the moon shines full at God's command, and all the stars obey.

Isaac Watts, 1674-1748, England

God thought that which did not exist, and by this thought brought it into being. At each moment we exist only because God consents to think us into being, although really we have no existence.

Simone Weil, 1909-1943, France

We assert that God's grace is manifest in all creation even though suffering, violence, and evil are everywhere present. The goodness of creation is fulfilled in human beings, who are called to covenant partnership with God. God has endowed us with dignity and freedom and has summoned us to responsibility for our lives and the life of the world.

The Book of Discipline of The United Methodist Church, 1992

I would not say that God is freedom or that God is love—even though the second pronouncement is a biblical one. We do not know what love is and we do not know what freedom is; but *God* is love and *God* is freedom. What freedom is and what love is, we have to learn from Him.

Karl Barth, 1886-1968, Switzerland

If we had only the first . . . words of the Creed, 'I believe in God the Father,' they would still be far beyond our understanding and reason.

Martin Luther, 1483-1546, Germany

There is an encompassing Mystery that grasps us and suffuses our existence and calls us into harmony with reality; that thwarts our unholy ventures (sooner or later); that haunts us, inspires us, reminds us of our mortality, snaps open shuttered glimpses of a reality that transcends what we know as nature, without decrying or negating any of nature's values or final goals.

Albert Outler, 1908-1989, United States

God saw everything that he had made, and indeed, it was very good.

Genesis 1:31

With God nothing is empty of meaning, nothing without symbolism.

Irenaeus, second century, Gaul

I believe; help my unbelief!

Mark 9:24

This is our Creator: in respect of his love, our Father, in respect of his power, our Lord, in respect of his wisdom, our Maker and Designer.

Irenaeus, second century, Gaul

33

CALLING TO
BAPTISM:

Professing
and Praying
with the
Church

O most high, omnipotent, good Lord God,
  to you belong praise, glory, honor, and all blessing.
For our brother the sun, who is our day and who brings us the light,
  who is fair, and radiant with a very great splendor;
For our sister the moon, and for the stars,
  which you have set clear and lovely in heaven;
For our brother the wind,
  and for air and clouds, calms and all weather;
For our sister water,
  who serves us and is humble and precious and chaste;
For our brother fire, by whom you light up the night,
  and who is fair and merry, and very mighty and strong;
For our mother the earth, who sustains us and keeps us,
  and brings forth various fruits,
  and flowers of many colors, and grass;
For all those who pardon one another for your love's sake,
  and who bear weakness and tribulation;
Blessed are they who peaceably shall endure,
  walking by your most holy will;
for you, O Most High, shall give them a crown.

Francis of Assisi, 1182–1226, Italy

The bud
stands for all things,
even for those things that don't flower,
for everything flowers, from within, of self-blessing;
though sometimes it is necessary
to reteach a thing its loveliness,
to put a hand on its brow
of the flower
and retell it in words and in touch
it is lovely
until it flowers again from within, of self-blessing;
as Saint Francis
put his hand on the creased forehead
of the sow, and told her in words and in touch
blessings of earth on the sow, and the sow
began remembering all down her thick length,
from the earthen snout all the way
through the fodder and slops to the spiritual curl of the tail,
from the hard spininess spiked out from the spine
down through the great broken heart
to the sheer blue milken dreaminess spurting and shuddering
from the fourteen teats into the fourteen mouths sucking and
  blowing beneath them:
the long, perfect loveliness of sow.

Galway Kinnell, United States

Gracious Voices

34

A Bird came down the walk:
He did not know I saw;
He bit an angle-worm in halves
And ate the fellow, raw.

And then he drank a dew
From a convenient grass,
And then he hopped sidewise to the wall
To let a beetle pass.

He glanced with rapid eyes
That hurried all abroad,—
They looked like frightened beads, I thought
He stirred his velvet head

Like one in danger; cautious,
I offered him a crumb,
And he unrolled his feathers
And rowed him softer home

Than oars divide the ocean,
Too silver for a seam,
Or butterflies, off banks of noon
Leap, plashless, as they swim.

Emily Dickinson, 1830-1886, United States

God is
that, the
greater
than which
cannot be
conceived.

Anselm,
1033-1109,
England

You know that the air and water are being polluted, as is everything we touch and live with, and we go on corrupting the nature
that we need. We don't realize we have a commitment to God to
take care of nature. To cut down a tree, to waste water when there
is so much lack of it, to let buses poison our atmosphere with
these noxious fumes from their exhausts, to burn rubbish haphaz-
ardly—all that concerns our alliance with God.

Oscar Romero, 1917-1980, El Salvador

God like a mother eagle hovers near
    on mighty wings of power manifest;
God like a gentle shepherd stills our fear,
    and comforts us against a peaceful breast.

C. Eric Lincoln, United States

CALLING TO
BAPTISM:

Professing
and Praying
with the
Church

I BELIEVE IN JESUS CHRIST, HIS ONLY SON, OUR LORD,

About noon I preached at Warrington; I am afraid, not to the taste of some of my hearers, as my subject led me to speak strongly and explicitly on the Godhead of Christ. But that I cannot help, for on this I *must* insist as the foundation of all our hope.

John Wesley, 1703-1791, England

I am the light of the world. Whoever follows me will never walk in darkness but will have the light of life.

John 8:12

Who was Jesus?

He was a storyteller.
He told stories. He was the world's greatest storyteller. Ask him a question; he'd answer with a story. Give him a crowd of people listening intently; he told them stories. Give him an argument; he'd give you a story. Give him a real tricky, catchy question: he'd give you a real tricky, catchy story.
Have you ever watched a seven-year-old listening—inhaling—a story? Eyes wide, mouth slung open, mind churning, he lives, accepts, and believes. He is totally absorbed.

This man-God Jesus. He was a good storyteller. He knew what he was doing.

Lois Cheney, United States

When we speak about wisdom, we are speaking of Christ. When we speak about virtue, we are speaking of Christ. When we speak about justice, we are speaking of Christ. When we speak about peace, we are speaking of Christ. When we speak about truth and life and redemption, we are speaking of Christ.

Ambrose of Milan, 340?-397

As no darkness can be seen by anyone surrounded by light, so no trivialities can capture the attention of anyone who has his eyes on Christ. The man who keeps his eyes upon the head and origin of the whole universe has them on virtue in all its perfection; he has them on truth, on justice, on immortality, and on everything else that is good, for Christ is goodness itself.

Gregory of Nyssa, 331?-394, Asia Minor

Gracious Voices

A mother's is the most intimate, willing, and dependable of all services, because it is the truest of all. None has been able to fulfill it properly but Christ, and he alone can. We know that our own mother's bearing of us was a bearing to pain and death, but what does Jesus, our true Mother, do? Why, he, All-love, bears us to joy and eternal life! Blessings on him!

Julian of Norwich, 1342?-?, England

I desire and choose poverty with Christ poor, rather than riches; insults with Christ loaded with them, rather than honors; I desire to be accounted as worthless and a fool for Christ rather than to be esteemed as wise and prudent in this world. So Christ was treated before me.

Ignatius of Loyola, 1491?-1556, Spain

Yes, of a truth he will be a king, but a poor and wretched king who has in no way the appearance of a king if He is judged by outward might and splendor, in which worldly kings and princes like to array themselves. He leaves to other kings such things as pomp, castles, palaces, gold, and wealth; and He lets them eat and drink, dress and build more daintily than other folks; but the craft which Christ the poor beggar-king knows, they do not know. He helps against not one sin only, but against all my sin; and not against my sin only, but against the whole world's sin. He comes to take away not sickness only, but death; and not my death only, but the whole world's death. This, says the Prophet, tell the daughter of Zion, that she be not offended at his mean advent; but shut your eyes and open your ears, and perceive not how He rides there so beggarly, but hearken to what is said and preached about this poor king. His wretchedness and poverty are manifest, for He comes riding on an ass like a beggar having neither saddle nor spurs. But that he will take from us sin, strangle death, endow us with eternal holiness, eternal bliss, and eternal life, this cannot be seen. Wherefore you must hear and believe.

Martin Luther, 1483-1546, Germany

Meekness was the method that Jesus used with the apostles. He put up with their ignorance and roughness and even their infidelity. He treated sinners with kindness and affection that caused some to be shocked, others to be scandalized, and still others to gain hope in God's mercy. Thus, he bade us to be gentle and humble of heart.

John Bosco, 1815-1888, Italy

Through Christ we see as in a mirror the spotless and excellent face of God.

Clement of Rome,
first century

CALLING TO
BAPTISM:

Professing
and Praying
with the
Church

You are the overflowing abyss of divinity.
Oh king of all kings most worthy,
Supreme emperor,
Illustrious prince,
Ruler of infinite sweetness,
Faithful protector.

You are the vivifying gem of humanity's nobility.
Craftsman of great skill,
Teacher of infinite patience,
Counselor of great wisdom,
Most kind guardian,
Most faithful friend.

You are the delicate taste of intimate sweetness.
Oh most delicate caresser,
Gentlest passion,
Most ardent lover,
Sweetest spouse,
Most pure pursuer.

You are the burgeoning blossom of natural beauty.
Oh most lovable brother,
Most beautiful youth,
Happiest companion,
Most munificent host,
Most courteous administrator.

Gertrude of Helfta, 1241-1298, Germany

The existence of the man Jesus Christ is, in virtue of his divinity,
the sovereign decision upon the existence of every man. It is based
on the fact that by God's dispensation this One stands for all and
so all are bound and obligated to this One. His community knows
this. This is what it has to make known to the world.

Karl Barth, 1886-1968, Switzerland

"The Spirit of the LORD is upon me,
  because he has anointed me
    to bring good news to the poor.
He has sent me to proclaim release to the captives
    and recovery of sight to the blind,
    to let the oppressed go free,
to proclaim the year of the Lord's favor."

Luke 4:18-19

Gracious Voices

38

For Jesus, broken bodies and empty bellies are the antithesis of God's reign; he embodies God's rule through healing broken bodies, filling empty bellies, and conducting himself in such a way that he is called a "winebibber and glutton."

Theodore Jennings, United States

The Greek acronym for some of the names of Christ yields *ichthys,* Christ as fish, and fish as Christ. The more I glimpse the fish in Tinker Creek, the more satisfying the coincidence becomes, the richer the symbol, not only for Christ but for the spirit as well. The people must live. Imagine for a Mediterranean people how much easier it is to haul up free, fed fish in nets than to pasture hungry herds on those bony hills and feed them through a winter. To say that holiness is a fish is a statement of the abundance of grace; it is the equivalent of affirming in a purely materialistic culture that money does indeed grow on trees. "Not as the world gives do I give to you"; these fish are spirit food. And revelation is a study in stalking: "Cast the net on the right side of the ship, and ye shall find."

Annie Dillard, United States

If you are asked, What do you mean when you say, "I believe in Jesus Christ"? answer: I mean by this that I believe that Jesus Christ, the true Son of God, has become my Lord. How? By freeing me from death, sin, hell, and all evil. For before I had no king and lord; the devil was our lord and king; blindness, death, sin, the flesh, and the world were our lords whom we served. Now they have all been driven out and in their stead there has been given to us the Lord Christ, who is the Lord of righteousness, salvation, and all good.

Martin Luther, 1483-1546, Germany

Lord Jesus Christ,
who hast said that thou art the Way, the Truth and the Life:
we pray thee suffer us not at any time to stray from thee,
who art the Way;
nor ever to distrust thy promises,
who art the Truth;
nor rest in any other thing than thee,
who art the Life;
for thou hast taught us what to believe, what to do,
and wherein to rest.

Desiderius Erasmus, 1466?-1536, Holland

Let anyone who is thirsty come to me, and let the one who believes in me drink. As the scripture has said, "Out of the believer's heart shall flow rivers of living water."

John 7:37-38

CALLING TO
BAPTISM:

Professing
and Praying
with the
Church

I say that Jesus Christ comes to men and women just where they are. There are not many people of whom that can be said.

If you, knowing nothing about music, were to go to a professor of music for lessons, the probability is that he would say: "Well—get through the earlier stages with someone else. Let somebody else teach you the five-finger exercises. Come to me later."

Not so with Jesus. He comes to men and women where they are. He comes to Simon, a blaspheming fisherman at his nets. He comes to Matthew, a traitorous and extortionate tax-collector, at his desk. . . . He comes to men just where they are. Not ignorance, not learning; not fancied superiorities nor inferiorities, can keep Him out. He comes to men and women just where they are. But He will not stay where they are!

He's marching to Zion. He wants men and women to march with Him. He has plans.

W. E. Sangster, 1900-1960, England

Lord Jesus Christ, pierce my soul with your love so that I may always long for you alone, who are the bread of angels and the fulfillment of the soul's deepest desires. May my heart always hunger and feed upon you, so that my soul may be filled with the sweetness of your presence. May my soul thirst for you, who are the source of life, wisdom, knowledge, light and all the riches of God our Father. May I always seek and find you, think upon you, speak to you and do all things for the honor and glory of your holy name. Be always my only hope, my peace, my refuge and my help in whom my heart is rooted so that I may never be separated from you.

attributed to Bonaventure, 1221-1274, Italy

Your speech is offensive, Lord. If you have to speak the truth, why can't you soften it a bit for delicate ears and tender tastes? Reality is vulgar. We hide our garbage in plastic cans and bury our cesspools beneath our lawns. We cover our sweat with aerosol spray and our bourbon breath with peppermint. When you speak, take a lesson from the professionals. Turn on the background music and avoid naked honesty as you would obscenity. Call sin an inadequate perception and call the morgue a slumber room. Fish do not enjoy reading seafood menus nor do canaries enjoy movies of cats. If you insist on stating the truth, you may run out of an audience.

Wilbur E. Rees, United States

Gracious Voices

WHO WAS CONCEIVED BY THE HOLY SPIRIT, BORN OF THE VIRGIN MARY,

Sing of Mary, pure and lowly, maiden mother, wise and mild.
Sing of God's own Son most holy, who became her little child.
Fairest child of fairest mother, God the Lord who came to earth,
Word made flesh, our very brother, takes our nature by his birth.

Sing of Jesus, son of Mary, in the home at Nazareth.
Toil and labor cannot weary love enduring unto death.
Constant was the love he gave her, though it drove him from her side,
forth to preach, and heal, and suffer, till on Calvary he died.

Joyful mother, full of gladness, in thine arms thy Lord was born.
Mournful mother, full of sadness, all thy heart with pain was torn.
Glorious mother, now rewarded, with a crown at Jesus' hand,
age to age thy name recorded shall be blest in every land.

Roland Ford Palmer, England/Canada

Moreover we proclaim the holy Virgin to be in strict truth the Mother of God. For inasmuch as he who was born of her was true God, she who bare the true God incarnate is the true Mother of God. For we hold that God was born of her, not implying that the divinity of the Word received from her the beginning of its being, but meaning that God the Word himself, who was begotten of the Father timelessly before the ages, and was with the Father and the Spirit without beginning and through eternity, took up his abode in these last days for the sake of our salvation in the Virgin's womb, and was without change made flesh and born of her. For the holy Virgin did not bear mere man but true God: and not mere God but God incarnate, Who did not bring down his body from Heaven, nor simply passed through the Virgin as a channel, but received from her flesh of like essence to our own. . . . For if the body had come down from heaven and had not partaken of our nature, what would have been the use of his becoming man? For the purpose of God the Word becoming man was that the very same nature, which had sinned and fallen and become corrupted, should triumph over the deceiving tyrant and so be freed from corruption.

John of Damascus, 675?-749, Syria

Invisible in his own nature he became visible in ours. Beyond our grasp, he chose to come within our grasp. Existing before time began, he began to exist at a moment in time. Incapable of suffering as God, he did not refuse to be a man, capable of suffering. Immortal, he chose to be subject to the laws of death.

Leo the Great, ?-461, Rome

Woman in the night, spent from giving birth, guard our precious light; peace is on the earth! Come and join the song, women, children, men; Jesus makes us free to live again.

Brian Wren, England

CALLING TO
BAPTISM:

Professing
and Praying
with the
Church

The great mystery of God's compassion is that in his compassion, in his entering with us into the condition of a slave, he reveals himself to us as God. His becoming a servant is not an exception to his being God. His self-emptying and humiliation are not a step away from his true nature. His becoming as we are and dying on a cross is not a temporary interruption of his divine existence. Rather, in the emptied and humbled Christ we encounter God, we see who God really is, we come to know his true divinity.

Henri J. M. Nouwen, 1932-1996, United States

"I, Mary, am the fact; God is the truth; but Jesus is fact and truth—he is reality. You cannot see the immortal truth till it is born in the flesh of the fact. And because all birth is a sundering of the flesh, fact and reality seem to go separate ways. But it is not really so; the feet that must walk this road were made of me. Only one Jesus is to die today—one person whom you know—the truth of God and the fact of Mary. This is reality. From the beginning of time until now, this is the only thing that has ever really happened. When you understand this you will understand all prophecies, and all history. . . ."

Dorothy Sayers, 1893-1957, England

Here, then, those wise thoughts with which our reason soars up towards heaven to seek out God in His own Majesty, and to probe out how He reigns there on high, are taken from us. The goal is fixed elsewhere, so that I should run from all the corners of the world to Bethlehem, to the stable and that manger where the babe lies, or to the Virgin's lap. Yes, that subdues reason.

Do not search what is too high for thee. But here it comes down before my eyes, so that I can see the babe there in His Mother's lap. There lies a human being who was born like any other child, and lives like any other child, and shows no other nature, manner, and work than any other human being, so that no heart could guess that the creature is the Creator. Where, then, are all the wise men? Who could ever have conceived this or thought it out? Reason must bow, and must confess her blindness in that she wants to climb to heaven to fathom the Divine, while she cannot see what lies before her eyes.

Martin Luther, 1483-1546, Germany

The Word was not degraded by receiving a body, so that he should seek to "receive" God's gift. Rather he deified what he put on; and, more than that, he bestowed this gift upon the race of men.

Athanasius, 293?-373, Egypt

The care of the Creator for his creatures is well known to us, and it explains why the Redeemer became incarnate.

It was consistent with his love not to leave the human race to go to perdition, from the moment he had constructed the universe and given existence to non-existent beings.

The Lord of the world did not consider it right to allow human beings, for love of whom everything had been made, to be besieged by sin and sold like slaves to death.

For this reason he assumed human form, hid his invisible nature under visible guise, and kept the visible nature free from the stain of sin.

Undoubtedly, it would have been easy for him to save the human race without assuming the garment of the flesh. He could have overthrown the power of death by a simple act of will. He could have made the father of that power, sin, disappear by exiling it from earth in such a way that no trace of it would remain on the earth.

Instead of that, he chose to demonstrate the holiness of his providential care.

To restore human beings he did not employ as his servants the angels and archangels, nor cause a piercing voice to resound from heaven. He preferred to build for himself a chamber in the womb of the Virgin and from there to come among us.

For this reason we think of him as man and adore him as God. Begotten of the Father before the beginning of time, he took of the Virgin a visible body. He is the being who is both new and pre-existent.

Theodoret, ?-457, Syria

Did you ever think, when you were a child, what fun it would be if your toys could come to life? Well, suppose you could really have brought them to life. Imagine turning a tin soldier into a real little man. It would involve turning the tin into flesh. And suppose the tin soldier did not like it. He is not interested in flesh; all he sees is that the tin is being spoiled. He thinks you are killing him. He will do everything he can do to prevent you. He will not be made into a man if he can help it.

What you would have done about that tin soldier I do not know. But what God did about us was this. The Second person in God, the Son, became human Himself: was born into the world as an actual man—a real man of a particular height, with hair of a particular color, speaking a particular language, weighing so many stone. The Eternal Being, who knows everything and who created the whole universe, became not only a man but (before that) a baby, and before that a fetus inside a Woman's body. If you want to get the hang of it, think of how you would like to become a slug or a crab.

C. S. Lewis, 1898-1963, England

For God's foolishness is wiser than human wisdom, and God's weakness is stronger than human strength.

1 Corinthians 1:25

CALLING TO
BAPTISM:

Professing
and Praying
with the
Church

Mary said,
"My soul magnifies the Lord,
    and my spirit rejoices in God my Savior,
for he has looked with favor on the lowliness of his servant.
    Surely, from now on all generations will call me blessed;
for the Mighty One has done great things for me,
    and holy is his name.
His mercy is for those who fear him
    from generation to generation.
He has shown strength with his arm;
    he has scattered the proud in the thoughts of their hearts.
He has brought down the powerful from their thrones,
    and lifted up the lowly;
he has filled the hungry with good things,
    and sent the rich away empty.
He has helped his servant Israel,
    in remembrance of his mercy,
according to the promise he made to our ancestors,
    to Abraham and to his descendants forever."

Luke 1:46-55

On one hand she was just a girl, an immature and frightened girl who had the good sense to believe what an angel told her in what seemed like a dream. On the other hand she was the mother of the son of God, with faith enough to move mountains, to sing about the victories of her son as if he were already at the right hand of his father instead of a dollop of cells in her womb. She was not like us. She *was* like us. She just wanted to thank God for visiting her, but she ended up bearing his son. She just wanted to be blessed in a small way, but she ended up singing revolution, singing the Lord's own upheaval and tumult. She was not like us. She *was* like us. When we allow God to be born in us there is no telling, no telling at all, what will come out.

Barbara Brown Taylor, United States

From the beginning, the Christian claim that Christ is "fully human and fully Divine" meant and means the effort to formulate the deeply-felt conviction that His person and life do not simply manifest the fullest possibilities of human nature evolving from within. In Him, we feel, we see beyond the world—"Jesus from the ground suspires" does not express all that the Incarnation means for us.

Evelyn Underhill, 1875-1941, England

Gracious Voices

SUFFERED UNDER PONTIUS PILATE,
WAS CRUCIFIED, DIED, AND WAS BURIED;
HE DESCENDED TO THE DEAD.

Christ's obedience . . . implied not only doing, but suffering; suffering the whole will of God, from the time he came into the world, till "He bore our sins in His own body upon the tree"; yea, till having made a full atonement for them, "He bowed His head, and gave up the ghost." This is usually termed the passive righteousness of Christ; the former, His active righteousness. But as the active and passive righteousness of Christ were never, in fact, separated from each other, so we never need separate them at all, either in speaking or even in thinking. And it is with regard to both these conjointly, that Jesus is called "the Lord our Righteousness."

John Wesley, 1703-1791, England

Fix your eyes on the Crucified and nothing else will be of much importance to you.

Lord,
you are calling me to come to you,
and I am coming to you—
not with any merits of my own
but only with your mercy.
I am begging you for this mercy
in virtue of your Son's most sweet blood.
    Blood!
    Blood!
Father,
into your hands I surrender my soul
and my spirit.

Catherine of Siena, 1347-1380, Italy

Teresa of Avila, 1515-1582, Spain

God created through love and for love. God did not create anything except love itself, and the means to love. He created love in all its forms. He created beings capable of love from all possible distances. Because no other could do it, he himself went to the greatest possible distance, the infinite distance. This infinite distance between God and God, this supreme tearing apart, this agony beyond all others, this marvel of love, is the crucifixion. Nothing can be further from God than that which has been made accursed.

Simone Weil, 1909-1943, France

We are accounted righteous before God only for the merit of our Lord and Savior Jesus Christ, by faith, and not for our own works or deservings. Wherefore, that we are justified by faith, only, is a most wholesome doctrine, and very full of comfort.

The Articles of Religion of the Methodist Church

CALLING TO
BAPTISM:

Professing
and Praying
with the
Church

Now I was as one awakened out of some troublesome sleep and dream, and listening to this heavenly sentence, I was as if I had heard it thus expounded to me; Sinner, thou thinkest that because of thy sins and infirmities I cannot save thy Soul; but behold my Son is by me, and upon him I look, and not on thee, and will deal with thee according as I am pleased with him: at this I was greatly lightened in my mind, and made to understand that God could justifie a sinner at any time; it was but looking upon Christ, and imputing his benefits to us, and the work was forthwith done.

John Bunyan, 1628-1688, England

I danced on the sabbath and I cured the lame,
the holy people said it was a shame;
they whipped and they stripped and they hung me high;
and they left me there on a cross to die.

I danced on a Friday and the sky turned black;
it's hard to dance with the devil on your back;
they buried my body and they thought I'd gone,
but I am the dance and I still go on.

They cut me down and I leapt up high,
I am the life that'll never never die;
I'll live in you if you'll live in me;
I am the Lord of the Dance, said he.

Dance, then, wherever you may be;
I am the Lord of the Dance, said he.
And I'll lead you all, wherever you may be,
and I'll lead you all in the dance, said he.

Sydney Carter, England

The Word which was in the beginning comes to us as the Word of incarnation (Christmas), the Word of the cross (Good Friday) and the Word of resurrection (Easter). These Words are one Word. The incarnate Lord is the crucified Lord. The crucified Lord is the risen Lord. There is only one Jesus Christ, the Lord. No one can isolate incarnation from crucifixion, crucifixion from resurrection. Crucifixion does not make sense apart from incarnation, the resurrection from crucifixion. Crucifixion is the ultimate depth of incarnation (Philippians 2:6-8) and resurrection is the "therefore" of crucifixion (verse 9).

Kosuke Koyama, Japan

I was raised up, a cross:
  I lifted up the Mighty King,
Lord of the Heavens:
  I dared not bend.
They pierced me with dark nails:
  the wounds are seen on me,
open gashes of hatred.
  Nor did I dare harm any of them.
They mocked us both together.
  I was all wet with blood,
drenched from the side of that Man
  after he had sent forth his spirit.
I had endured many bitter happenings on that hill.
  I saw the God of Hosts cruelly racked.
The shades of night had covered the Ruler's body with their mists,
the bright splendor.
  Shadow came forth, dark beneath the clouds.
All creation wept, bewailed the King's fall; Christ was on Cross.

Dream of the Rood, Medieval poem

Every time in history that man has tried to turn crucified truth
into coercive truth he has betrayed the fundamental principle of
Christianity.

Nicolas Berdyaev, 1874-1948, Russia

Almighty God,
  your Son Jesus Christ was lifted high upon the cross
    so that he might draw the whole world to himself.
Grant that we, who glory in his death for our salvation,
  may also glory in his call to take up our cross and follow him;
through Jesus Christ our Lord. Amen.

Collect for Good Friday

Take thought now, redeemed man, and consider how great and
worthy is he who hangs on the cross for you. His death brings the
dead to life, but at his passing heaven and earth are plunged into
mourning and hard rocks are split asunder.

attributed to Bonaventure, 1221-1274, Italy

Out of love the Lord took us to himself; because he loved us and
it was God's will, our Lord Jesus Christ gave his life's blood for
us—he gave his body for our body, his soul for our soul.

Clement of Rome, first century

As through a tree we were made debtors to God, so through a tree we receive cancella-tion of our debt.

Irenaeus, second century, Gaul

CALLING TO
BAPTISM:

Professing
and Praying
with the
Church

Where have your love, your mercy, your compassion shone out more luminously than in your wounds, sweet gentle Lord of mercy? More mercy than this no one has than that he lay down his life for those who are doomed to death.

Bernard of Clairvaux, 1090-1153, France

Soul of Christ, sanctify me.
Body of Christ, save me.
Blood of Christ, inebriate me.
Water from the side of Christ, wash me.
Passion of Christ, strengthen me.
O good Jesus, hear me;
Within thy wounds hide me;
Suffer me not to be separated from thee;
From the malignant enemy defend me;
In the hour of my death call me,
And bid me come to thee,
That with thy saints I may praise thee
Forever and ever. Amen.

Ignatius Loyola, 1491?-1556, Spain

Too often, American evangelical Christianity presents the good news of Christ as the solution for all human problems, the fulfill-ment of all our wants, a good way to make basically good people even better. But the cross suggests that the good news is the begin-ning of problems, the turning away from our quest for self-fulfill-ment, the ultimate mocking of our delusions of goodness. Nothing less than death will do. Nothing less than deadly, painful, full-scale conversion—turning around from ourselves toward God and others.

Christianity is a thing of great comfort. But it does not begin in comfort; it begins in some pain. We cannot ask for the comfort before we face the cross. The cross reminds us that God gains vic-tories through pain rather than through force, through self-giving rather than self-seeking. Our victories come the same way.

William Willimon, United States

To mock your reign, O dearest Lord,
they made a crown of thorns;
set you with taunts along that road
from which no one returns.
They could not know, as we do now, how glorious is that crown;
that thorns would flower upon your brow,
your sorrows heal our own.

Fred Pratt Green, England

Wilt thou love God, as he thee? then digest,
My Soule, this wholsome meditation,
How God the Spirit, by Angels waited on
In heaven, doth make his Temple in thy brest.
The Father having begot a Sonne most blest,
And still begetting, (for he ne'r begonne)
Hath deign'd to chuse thee by adoption,
Coheire to 'his glory,' and Sabbaths endlessse rest;
And as a robb'd man, which by search doth finde
His stolne stuffe sold, must lose or buy'it againe:
The Sonne of glory came downe, and was slaine,
Us whom he'had made, and Satan stolne, to unbinde.
'Twas much, that man was made like God before,
But, that God should be made like man, much more.

John Donne, 1573-1631, England

The main thing, of course, is to love, even to the folly of the Cross.
In the Book of Hosea in the Old Testament, the picture of God's
love is the picture of the prophet loving his harlot wife, and supporting not only her but her lovers. What foolish love, what unjudg-
ing love! And the picture of God's love in the New Testament is of
Christ, our Brother, dying for us on the Cross, for us who are
ungrateful, undeserving. Let us love God, since He first loved us.
And let us show our love for God by our love for neighbor.

Dorothy Day, 1897-1980, United States

What takes place in the crucifixion of Christ is that God's Son
takes to Himself that which must come to the creature existing in
revolt, which wants to deliver itself from its creatureliness and itself
be the Creator. He puts himself into this creature's need and does
not abandon it to itself. Moreover, He does not only help it from
without and greet it only from afar off; He makes the misery of His
creature His own. To what end? So that His creature may go out
freely, so that the burden which it has laid upon itself may be
borne, borne away. The creature itself must have gone to pieces,
but God does not want that; He wants it to be saved. So great is
the ruin of the creature that less than the self-surrender of God
would not suffice for its rescue. But so great is God, that it is His
will to render up Himself. Reconciliation means God taking man's
place. Let me add that no doctrine of this central mystery can
exhaustively and precisely grasp and express the extent to which
God has intervened for us here. Do not confuse my theory of the
reconciliation with the thing itself. All theories of reconciliation
can be but pointers. But do also pay attention to this 'for us': nothing must be deducted from it! Whatever a doctrine of reconciliation tries to express, it *must* say this.

Karl Barth, 1886-1968, Switzerland

Here is the
Lamb of
God who
takes away
the sin of
the world!

John 1:29

CALLING TO
BAPTISM:

Professing
and Praying
with the
Church

O Christ, upon whom the many-eyed cherubim
are unable to look
because of the glory of your face
yet out of your love
you received spit upon your face;
remove the shame from my face,
and grant me an open face before you
at the time of prayer.

Isaac of Nineveh, seventh century, East Syria

He breaks the power of canceled sin,
he sets the prisoner free;
his blood can make the foulest clean;
his blood availed for me.

Charles Wesley, 1707-1788, England

Jesus truly suffered for all. For the Cross was no illusion; otherwise our redemption also is an illusion. His death was not imaginary; otherwise our salvation is an idle tale. If His death was imaginary, they were right who said: "We have remembered how that deceiver said, while he was yet alive, 'After three days I will rise again.' " Therefore his passion was real, for He was truly crucified, and we are not ashamed of it. He was crucified and we do not deny it, but rather do I glory in speaking of it. For if I should now deny it, Golgotha here, close to which we are now gathered, refutes me. . . . I confess the Cross, because I know of the Resurrection; had the Cross been the end, perhaps I would not have confessed it, but concealed both it and my Master; however, since the Cross was followed by the Resurrection, I am not ashamed to avow it.

Cyril of Jerusalem, 313?-386

Fellowship with Christ cannot normally be secured in the church by exalting his person at the expense of his atonement. It verily seems as if the whole realm of Christian scholarship were trying to minimize the death of the Son of God. The tendency is not only wrong, but even pernicious. Fully to enter into the life of Christ, one needs to be overwhelmed by his death as Saint Paul was overwhelmed by it until he could hardly think a thought which was not colored by its sacrificial meaning.

Olin A. Curtis, 1850-1918, United States

Gracious Voices

By his first work He gave me to myself; and by the next He gave Himself to me. And when He gave Himself, He gave me back myself that I had lost.

Bernard of Clairvaux, 1090-1153, France

If two men were to eat nuts together, and the one liked only the shell, the other only the kernel, one may say that they match one another well. What the world rejects, casts away, despises, namely, the sacrificed man, the kernel—precisely upon that God sets the greatest store, and treasures it with greater zeal than does the world that which it loves with the greatest passion.

Søren Kierkegaard, 1813-1855, Denmark

I am the good shepherd. The good shepherd lays down his life for the sheep.

John 10:11

Yea, truly blessed! For this King and His Word, in which people should find great joy, are a stumbling-block for all the world. The world takes offence and is provoked by the Gospel of Christ, because it will not trust in the grace of God, but rather in its own works and merits. And again the world takes offence at Christ because He is so utterly poor and wretched. And again, that, as He carries His cross and lets himself be hanged upon it, He admonishes His followers to take their cross and to follow Him through all manner of temptations and afflictions. To this the world is especially hostile.

Thus is our dear Lord Christ everywhere in the world an annoying preacher. The Gospel will never fare otherwise. It is and it will be a message at which offence is taken, not by the lowly, but by the most saintly and the most pious, the wisest and the mightiest on earth, as experience teaches us. Blessed are those who know and trust that it is truly the Word of God, for they are healed, and they are comforted and fortified against all such offence.

Martin Luther, 1483-1546, Germany

This, therefore, is the general ground of the whole doctrine of justification. By the sin of the first Adam, who was not only the father, but likewise the representative, of us all, we all fall short of the favor of God; we all became children of wrath; or, as the Apostle expresses it, "judgment came upon all men to condemnation." Even so, by the sacrifice for sin made by the second Adam, as the representative of us all, God is so far reconciled to all the world, that He hath given them a new covenant; the plain condition whereof being once fulfilled, "there is no more condemnation" for us, but "we are justified freely by His grace, through the redemption that is in Jesus Christ."

John Wesley, 1703-1791, England

The cup had been poured for Communion. I stood behind the Lord's table with my arms outstretched to pray the prayer of thanksgiving. "Look, Mommie," one of our younger members exclaimed. "He's trying to look like Jesus on the cross."

It's not a bad thing to say about a Christian.

William Willimon, United States

CALLING TO
BAPTISM:

Professing
and Praying
with the
Church

Jesus learned obedience from what he suffered. This means that the pains and struggles of which Jesus became part made him listen more perfectly to God. In and through his sufferings, he came to know God and could respond to his call. Maybe there are no better words than these to summarize the meaning of the option for the poor. Entering into the suffering of the poor is the way to become obedient, that is, a listener to God. Suffering accepted and shared in love breaks down our selfish defenses and sets us free to accept God's guidance.

Henri J. M. Nouwen, 1932-1996, United States

What one of us can understand a love so great that we would willingly limit our unlimitedness, put the flesh of mortality over our immortality, accept all the pain and grief of humanity, submit to betrayal by that humanity, be killed by it, and die a total failure (in human terms) on a common cross between two thieves?

Madeleine L'Engle, United States

It is none other than Jesus Christ himself who suffered the scandalous, public death of a sinner in our stead. He was not ashamed to be crucified for us as an evildoer. It is nothing else but our fellowship with Jesus Christ that leads us to that ignominious dying that comes in confession [of sin], in order that we may in truth share in his Cross. The Cross of Jesus Christ destroys all pride. We cannot find the Cross of Jesus if we shrink from going to the place where it is to be found, namely, the public death of the sinner. And we refuse to bear the Cross when we are ashamed to take upon ourselves the shameful death of the sinner in confession. In confession we break through to the true fellowship of the Cross of Jesus Christ, in confession we affirm and accept our cross. In the deep mental and physical pain of humiliation before a [brother or sister]—which means, before God—we experience the Cross of Jesus as our rescue and salvation. The old man dies, but it is God who has conquered him. Now we share in the resurrection of Christ and eternal life.

Dietrich Bonhoeffer, 1906-1945, Germany

For while we were still weak, at the right time Christ died for the ungodly. Indeed, rarely will anyone die for a righteous person—though perhaps for a good person someone might actually dare to die. But God proves his love for us in that while we were yet sinners Christ died for us.

Romans 5:6-8

ON THE THIRD DAY HE ROSE AGAIN;
HE ASCENDED INTO HEAVEN,
IS SEATED AT THE RIGHT HAND OF THE FATHER,
AND WILL COME AGAIN TO JUDGE THE
LIVING AND THE DEAD.

Christ the Lord is risen today, Alleluia!
Earth and heaven in chorus say, Alleluia!
Raise your joys and triumphs high, Alleluia!
Sing, ye heavens, and earth reply, Alleluia!

Love's redeeming work is done, Alleluia!
Fought the fight, the battle won, Alleluia!
Death in vain forbids him rise, Alleluia!
Christ has opened paradise, Alleluia!

Lives again our glorious King, Alleluia!
Where, O death, is now thy sting? Alleluia!
Once he died our souls to save, Alleluia!
Where's thy victory, boasting grave? Alleluia!

Charles Wesley, 1707-1788, England

I will sing to the LORD, for he has triumphed gloriously;
   horse and rider he has thrown into the sea.
The LORD is my strength and my might,
   and he has become my salvation;
this is my God, and I will praise him,
   my father's God, and I will exalt him.
The LORD is a warrior;
   the LORD is his name.

Exodus 15:1-3

How inexhaustibly rich the Easter event is! What astonishing
proclamation we make. Death is vanquished! Sin is overcome!
Creation itself becomes a font of blessings! A new covenant is
trothed! For a day we live liturgically into the truths that we
glimpsed off and on during the Lenten season. God's reign of justice and peace becomes ours. Mercy overflows. Wounds are
healed. Love, tender and limitless and astonishing, embraces us. It
is the custom of the Christian community in Tanzania at the close
of the vigil to dance until the coming of the Easter dawn. What
better way to celebrate the feast of feasts: to dance for sheer joy!

Wendy Wright, United States

God did
not abolish
the fact of
evil: He
trans-
formed it.
He did not
stop the
crucifixion:
He rose
from the
dead.

Dorothy Sayers,
1893-1957,
England

CALLING TO BAPTISM:

Professing and Praying with the Church

I look at Thee, my Lord Jesus, and think of Thy Most Holy Body, and I keep it before me as the pledge of my own resurrection. Though I die, as die I certainly shall, nevertheless I shall not for ever die, for I shall rise again. My Lord, the heathen who knew thee not, thought the body to be of a miserable and contemptible nature—they thought it the seat, the cause, the excuse of all moral evil. When their thoughts soared highest, and they thought of a future life, they considered that the destruction of the body was the condition of that higher existence. That the body was really part of themselves and that its restoration could be a privilege, was beyond their utmost imagination. And indeed, what mind of man, O Lord, could ever have fancied without thy revelation that what, according to our experience, is so vile, so degraded, so animal, so sinful, which is our fellowship with the brutes, which is full of corruption and becomes dust and ashes, was in its very nature capable of so high a destiny! that it could become celestial and immortal, without ceasing to be a body! And who but thou, who art omnipotent, could have made it so! No wonder then, that the wise men of the world, who did not believe in Thee, scoffed at the Resurrection. But I, by Thy grace, will ever keep before me how differently I have been taught by Thee. O best and first and truest of Teachers! O Thou who art the Truth, I know, and believe with my whole heart, that this very flesh of mine will rise again. I know, base and odious as it is at present, that it will one day, if I be worthy, be raised incorruptible and altogether beautiful and glorious. This I know; this, by thy grace, I will ever keep before me.

John Henry Newman, 1801-1890, England

Lord, in these times when we are about to lose hope and our efforts seem futile, grant that we may perceive in our hearts and minds the image of your resurrection which remains our only source of courage and strength, so that we may continue to face the challenges, and struggle against hardship and oppression born of injustice.

from a liturgy created for use by the people of one of the poorest slum areas of Manila

Clean out the old yeast so that you may be a new batch, as you really are unleavened. For our paschal lamb, Christ, has been sacrificed. Therefore, let us celebrate the festival, not with the old yeast, the yeast of malice and evil, but with the unleavened bread of sincerity and truth.

1 Corinthians 5:7-8

Gracious Voices

Glory to the Father, who has woven garments
   of glory for the resurrection.
Worship to the Son, who was clothed in them at his rising.
Thanksgiving to the Spirit, who keeps them for all the saints.

Syrian Orthodox Liturgy

For I know that my Redeemer lives,
    and that at the last he will stand upon the earth;
and after my skin has been thus destroyed,
    then in my flesh I shall see God,
whom I shall see on my side,
    and my eyes shall behold, and not another.
My heart faints within me!

Job 19:25-27

There is a general connection of *all* people with Christ, and every
person is His brother. He died for everyone and rose for all; so
everyone is the addressee of the work of Jesus Christ. That this is
the case, is a promise for the whole of humanity. And it is the most
important basis, and the only one which touches everything, for
what we call humanity. He who has once realized the fact that
God was made man cannot speak and act inhumanely.

Karl Barth, 1886-1968, Switzerland

God has gone up with a shout,
    the LORD with the sound of a trumpet.
Sing praises to God, sing praises;
    sing praises to our King, sing praises.

Psalm 47:5-6

Before He entered through the closed doors he was sought by
those noble and courageous women; He was sought, the
Bridegroom and Suitor of souls. These blessed women came to the
sepulchre and sought Him who was risen; and tears were still
flowing from their eyes, though it was more fitting for them to
dance with joy for Him who had risen. . . .

Recall also what I have often said regarding the sitting of the
Son at the right hand of the Father, according to the sequence of
the Creed: "and he ascended into heaven, and sits at the right
hand of the Father." Let us not too curiously inquire into the pre-
cise nature of this sitting, for it surpasses our understanding.

Cyril of Jerusalem, 313?-386

The New Testament writers speak as if Christ's achievement in rising from the dead was the first event of its kind in the whole history
of the universe. He is the "first fruits," the "pioneer of life." He has
forced open a door that has been locked since the death of the first
man. He has met, fought, and beaten the King of Death. Everything
is different because He has done so. This is the beginning of the
New Creation: a new chapter in cosmic history has opened.

C. S. Lewis, 1898-1963, England

Your righteous-
ness is like
the mighty
mountains,
your
judgments
are like
the great
deep;
you save
humans
and
animals
alike,
O LORD.

Psalm 36:6

CALLING TO
BAPTISM:

Professing
and Praying
with the
Church

For a little while we have lived back in
The enchanted world of childhood, But now
Someone has taken down the wonderful
Christmas tree, put all the bright toys away.
The children are back in school, robbing us
Of their annoying, glorious laughter.
It seems as though all the furniture has
Been moved out of the house, We have nothing
To do but sit on the bare floor looking
Out of the window at the dead of Winter.
Tomorrow is the old age that lies like
The charred tree next to the rubbish barrel.
The three long months of Winter are the Three
Days that begin with Good Friday. By then
Another tree will be taken down with
A Man stretched across it. On the Third day
He will melt the January ice in
Our souls and make us children forever.

A. Roy Eckardt, United States

Hail thee, festival day! blest day to be hallowed forever;
day when our risen Lord rose in the heavens to reign.
He who was nailed to the cross
is Ruler and Lord of all people.
All things created on earth
sing to the glory of God:
Daily the loveliness grows,
adorned with the glory of blossom;
heaven her gates unbars,
flinging her increase of light.

Venantius Honorius Fortunatus, 530-609, France

The Ascension of Christ was very beneficial for us. This is seen in
three ways. First, as our Leader, because he ascended in order to
lead us; for we had lost the way, but He has shown it to us. "For
He shall go up that shall open the way before them," (Micah 2:13)
and thus we may be made certain of possessing the heavenly kingdom: "I go to prepare a place for you" (John 14:2). Secondly, that
he might draw our hearts to Himself: "For where thy treasure is,
there is thy heart also" (Matthew 6:21). Thirdly, to let us withdraw
from worldly things: "Therefore, if you have been risen with Christ,
seek the things that are above, where Christ is sitting at the right
hand of God. Mind the things that are above, not the things that
are upon the earth" (Colossians 3:1).

Thomas Aquinas, 1227?-1274?, Italy

Gracious Voices

If we are worth anything,
   it is not because we have more money
   or more talent
   or more human qualities.
Insofar as we are worth anything,
   it is because we are grafted onto Christ's life,
   to his cross and resurrection.
   That is a persons measure.

Oscar Romero, 1917-1980, El Salvador

Here then we see in the clearest, strongest light, what is real religion: A restoration of man by Him that bruises the serpent's head, to all that the old serpent deprived him of; a restoration, not only to the favor but likewise to the image of God, implying not barely deliverance from sin, but the being filled with the fulness of God. It is plain, if we attend to the preceding considerations, that nothing short of this is Christian religion. Every thing else, whether negative or external, is utterly wide of the mark.

John Wesley, 1703-1791, England

Since, then, we have a great high priest who has passed through the heavens, Jesus, the Son of God, let us hold fast to our confession. For we do not have a high priest who is unable to sympathize with our weaknesses, but we have one who in every respect has been tested as we are, yet without sin. Let us therefore approach the throne of grace with boldness, so that we may receive mercy and find grace to help in time of need.

Hebrews 4:14-16

Life and death, words and silence, are given us because of Christ. In Christ we die to the flesh and live to the spirit. In Him we die to illusion and live to truth. We speak to confess Him, and we are silent in order to meditate on Him and enter deeper into His silence, which is at once the silence of death and of eternal life— the silence of Good Friday night and the peace of Easter morning.

Thomas Merton, 1915-1968, United States

I am happy because you have accepted me, dear Lord.
Sometimes I do not know what to do with all my happiness.
I swim in your grace like a whale in the ocean.
The saying goes: "An ocean never dries up,"
but we know that your grace also never fails.
Dear Lord, your grace is our happiness. Hallelujah!

a prayer from West Africa

May I never boast of anything except the cross of our Lord Jesus Christ, by which the world has been crucified to me, and I to the world.

Galatians 6:14

CALLING TO
BAPTISM:

Professing
and Praying
with the
Church

I BELIEVE IN THE HOLY SPIRIT,

The Holy Ghost also helped to make us Christians. . . . the Holy Ghost comes in baptism to form Jesus Christ in our souls, to incorporate us, to give us birth and make us live in Christ, to apply to us the infinite merits of His Precious Blood and His death, and to animate, inspire and direct us in all we think, say, do and suffer as Christians and for God; therefore we cannot pronounce the name of Jesus except by the power of the Holy Ghost, and we are not sufficient to think a holy thought without the grace of God.

John Eudes, 1601-1680, France

The fruit of the Spirit is love, joy, peace, patience, kindness, generosity, faithfulness, gentleness, and self-control. There is no law against such things. And those who belong to Christ Jesus have crucified the flesh with its passions and desires. If we live by the Spirit, let us also be guided by the Spirit. Let us not become conceited, competing against one another, envying one another.

Galatians 5:22-26

The Holy Ghost, proceeding from the Father and the Son, is of one substance, majesty, and glory with the Father and the Son, very and eternal God.

The Articles of Religion of The Methodist Church

Like the murmur of the dove's song,
like the challenge of her flight,
like the vigor of the wind's rush,
like the new flame's eager might:
Come, Holy Spirit, come.
To the members of Christ's body,
to the branches of the Vine,
to the church in faith assembled,
to her midst as gift and sign:
Come, Holy Spirit, come.

With the healing of division,
with the ceaseless voice of prayer,
with the power to love and witness,
with the peace beyond compare:
Come, Holy Spirit, come.

Carl P. Daw, Jr., United States

Gracious Voices

I adore thee, O my Lord, the Third Person of the All-Blessed Trinity, that thou hast set up in this world of sin a great light upon a hill. Thou hast founded the Church, Thou hast established and maintained it. Thou fillest it continually with Thy gifts, that men may see, and draw near, and take, and live. . . .

I adore Thee, O Almighty Lord, the Paraclete, because Thou in Thy infinite compassion hast brought me into this Church, the work of Thy supernatural power. I had no claim on Thee for so wonderful a favor over anyone else in the whole world. There were many men far better than I by nature, gifted with more pleasing natural gifts, and less stained with sin. Yet Thou, in Thy inscrutable love for me, hast chosen me and brought me into Thy fold. Thou hast a reason for everything Thou dost. I know there must have been an all-wise reason, as we speak in human language, for Thy choosing me and not another—but I know that that reason was something external to myself. I did nothing towards it—I did everything against it. I did everything to thwart Thy purpose. And thus I owed all to Thy grace. I should have lived and died in darkness and sin; I should have become worse and worse the longer I lived; I should have got more to hate and abjure Thee, O Source of my bliss; I should have got yearly more fit for hell, and at length I should have gone there, but for Thy incomprehensible love to me. O my God, that overpowering love took me captive. Was any boyhood so impious as some years of mine! Did I not in fact dare Thee to do Thy worst? Ah, how I struggled to get free from thee; but Thou art stronger than I and hast prevailed. I have not a word to say, but to bow down in awe before the depths of Thy love.

John Henry Newman, 1801-1890, England

It is the Holy Spirit, dwelling in those who believe and pervading and ruling over the entire Church, who brings about that wonderful communion of the faithful and joins them together so intimately in Christ that he is the principle of the Church's unity. By distributing various kinds of spiritual gifts and ministries, he enriches the Church of Jesus Christ with different functions "in order to equip the saints for the work of service, so as to build up the body of Christ."

Vatican Council II, 1962-1965

Christ died and so deserved our love. The Holy Spirit works on us and makes us love him. Christ has given us a reason for loving him; the Spirit has given us the power to love him. The one commends his great love to us; the other gives it. In the one we see the object of our love; by the other we have the power to love. The former provides the occasion of our love; the latter provides the love itself.

Bernard of Clairvaux, 1090-1153, France

Now there are a variety of gifts, but the same Spirit; and there are varieties of service, but the same Lord; ...To each is given the manifestation of the Spirit for the common good.

1 Corinthians 12:4-7

CALLING TO
BAPTISM:

Professing
and Praying
with the
Church

O living flame of love
That tenderly wounds my soul
In its deepest center! Since
Now you are not oppressive,
Now Consummate! if it be your will:
Tear through the veil of this sweet encounter.
O sweet cautery
O delightful wound!
O gentle hand! O delicate touch
That tastes of eternal life
And pays every debt!
In killing you changed death to life.

O lamp of fire!
In whose splendors
The deep caverns of feeling,
Once obscure and blind,
Now give forth, so rarely, so exquisitely,
Both warmth and light to their beloved.

How gently and lovingly
You wake in my heart,
Where in secret you dwell alone;
And in your sweet breathing,
Filled with good and glory,
How tenderly you swell my heart with love.

John of the Cross, 1542-1591, Spain

Sanctification is that renewal of our fallen nature by the Holy Ghost, received through faith in Jesus Christ, whose blood of atonement cleanseth from all sin; whereby we are not only delivered from the guilt of sin, but are washed from its pollution, saved from its power, and are enabled, through grace, to love God with all our hearts and to walk in his holy commandments blameless.

The Articles of Religion of The Methodist Church

O Holy Ghost, that givest grace where Thou wilt, come into me and ravish me to Thyself. The nature that Thou didst make, change with honeysweet gifts, that my soul, filled with Thy delightful joy, may despise and cast away all the things of this world, that it may receive ghostly gifts, given by Thee, and going with joyful songs into infinite light may be all melted in holy love.

attributed to Richard Rolle, 1300?-1349, England

Come, Holy Ghost, our souls inspire,
and lighten with celestial fire;
thou the anointing Spirit art,
who dost thy sevenfold gifts impart.

Thy blessed unction from above
is comfort, life, and fire of love;
enable with perpetual light
the dullness of our blinded sight.

Anoint and cheer our soiled face
with the abundance of thy grace;
keep far our foes; give peace at home;
where thou art guide, no ill can come.

attributed to Rhabanus Maurus, 776-856, Germany

The Holy Spirit's. . . actions . . . effect what is good and salutary.
First of all, His coming is gentle, the perception of him fragrant,
His yoke light; rays of light and knowledge shine forth before his
coming. He comes with the heart of a true guardian; He comes to
save, to cure, to admonish, to strengthen, to console, to enlighten
the mind, first of the one who receives Him, then through that one
to the minds of others also.

Cyril of Jerusalem, 313?-386

To know when we are hearing the voice of the Holy Spirit, and
when we are listening to our own unhallowed subconscious
impulses, is not an easy matter. There are indices and channels of
discovery in an unbiased and comprehensive survey of the total
situation, in corporate worship that is deep and genuine, in inter-
change of thought with other wise and well-grounded Christians,
in prayer and commitment that carries with it a willingness to go
where the Spirit leads. Yet there is one safeguard that is indispens-
able to all others. It is what Paul calls the mind of Christ. Whatever
carries forward our understanding of God and of his will as this
has been revealed to us in Jesus *is* the work of the Holy Spirit; all
else is suspect.

Georgia Harkness, 1891-1974, United States

"Life in the Spirit" involves diligent use of the means of grace
such as praying, fasting, attending upon the Sacraments, and
inward searching in solitude. It also encompasses the communal
life of the Church in worship, mission, evangelism, service, and
social witness.

The Book of Discipline of The United Methodist Church, 1992

The Holy Spirit work within you, that being born through water and the Spirit, you may be a faith-ful disciple of Jesus Christ.

Laying on of Hands, Baptismal Covenant

CALLING TO
BAPTISM:

Professing
and Praying
with the
Church

Peace of conscience and joy in the Holy Ghost must proceed from the indwelling of that Holy Spirit; and those who have these blessings must know that they have them, for we cannot have heavenly peace and heavenly joy without knowing that we have them. But this Spirit in the soul of a believer is not only manifest by its effects, but it bears its own witness to its own indwelling. So that one not only knows that he has the Spirit from the fruits of the Spirit, but he knows that he has it from its own direct witness. It may be said, "How can these things be?" And it may be answered, "By the power, light, and mercy of God." But that such things are, the Scriptures uniformly attest; and the experience of the whole genuine church of Christ, and of every truly converted soul, sufficiently proves. "As the wind bloweth where it will," and we "cannot tell whence it cometh and whither it goeth, so is every one that is born of the Spirit." The thing is certain, and fully known by its effects; but how this testimony is given and confirmed, is inexplicable. Every good person feels it, and knows he is of God by the Spirit God has given him.

Adam Clark, 1760?-1832, Ireland

Who is the third who always walks beside you?
When I count, there are only you and I together
But when I look ahead up the white road
There is always another one walking beside you.

T. S. Eliot, 1888-1965, England

Will you be faithful in prayer,
in the reading and study of the Holy Scriptures,
and with the help of the Holy Spirit
continually rekindle the gift of God that is in you?

Examination, The Order for the Ordination of Deacons

I'm goin' a sing when the Spirit says sing,
I'm goin' a sing when the Spirit says sing,
I'm goin' a sing when the Spirit says sing,
and obey the Spirit of the Lord.

African American spiritual

Brothers and sisters,
from time to time we experience a new beginning
in our faith journey,
when the Holy Spirit breaks into our lives to
inspire us, to lead us,
and to deepen our commitment to Christ.

Service for A Celebration of New Beginnings in Faith

Gracious Voices

I believe that I cannot by my own reason or strength believe in Jesus Christ my Lord, or come to him; but the Holy Ghost has called me through the gospel, enlightened me, and sanctified and preserved me in the true faith; in like manner as he calls, gathers, enlightens and sanctifies the whole Christian Church on earth, and preserves it in union with Jesus Christ in the true faith; in which Christian Church the Holy Ghost daily forgives abundantly all my sins, and the sins of all believers, and will raise me up and all the dead at the last day, and will grant everlasting life to me and to all who believe in Christ. This is most certainly true. Amen.

Martin Luther, 1483-1546, Germany

O Great Spirit
  whose voice we hear in the winds,
  and whose breath gives life to all the world, hear us.
We come before you as your children.
We are small and weak; we need your strength and wisdom.
Let us walk in beauty
  and make our eyes ever behold the red and purple sunset.
May our hands respect the things you have made,
  our ears be sharp to hear your voice.
Make us wise,
  so that we may know the things you have taught your people,
  the lessons you have hidden in every leaf and rock.
We seek strength not to be superior to our brothers and sisters,
  but to live in harmony with ourselves and all of your creation.
Help us to be ever ready to come to you,
  so when life fades as a fading sunset,
  our spirits may come to you without shame. Amen.

Native American prayer

The Holy Spirit rests in the soul of the just like a dove in her nest. He hatches good desires in a pure soul, as the dove hatches her young.

attributed to John Vianney, 1786-1859, France

We know there have been fashionable objections to females praying in public, but I am sure I do not exaggerate when I say I have often seen our dull and stupid prayer-meetings suddenly change from a dead clog to a heavenly enjoyment, when a sister has been called on to pray, who has reverently bowed and taken up the cross, and utterance was given her that was heavenly, and she prayed with words that burned, and the baptismal fire rolled all around, while the house and all the praying company were baptized from heaven, many sinners, tall and stout-hearted sinners, have been brought to quake and tremble before God, and have cried for mercy, and while crying have found peace with God through our Lord Jesus Christ.

Peter Cartwright, 1785-1872, United States

CALLING TO
BAPTISM:

Professing
and Praying
with the
Church

THE HOLY CATHOLIC CHURCH,

The church is of God,
and will be preserved to the end of time,
for the conduct of worship
   and the due administration of God's Word and Sacraments,
the maintenance of Christian fellowship and discipline,
the edification of believers,
and the conversion of the world.
All, of every age and station,
   stand in need of the means of grace which it alone supplies.

Introduction, Baptismal Covenant

The church is one which with increasing fecundity extends far
and wide into the multitude, just as the rays of the sun are many
but the light is one, and the branches of the tree are many but the
strength is one founded in its tenacious root, and, when many
streams flow from one source, although a multiplicity of water
seems to have been diffused from the abundance of the overflowing supply nevertheless unity is preserved in their origin. Take
away a ray of light from the body of the sun, its unity does not take
on any division of its light; break a branch from a tree, the branch
thus broken will not be able to bud; cut off a stream from its
source, the stream thus cut off dries up. Thus too the church
bathed in the light of the Lord projects its rays over the whole
world, yet there is one light which is diffused everywhere, and the
unity of the body is not separated. She extends her branches over
the whole earth in fruitful abundance; she extends her richly flowing streams far and wide; yet her head is one, and her source is
one, and she is the one mother copious in the results of her fruit-
fulness. By her womb we are born; by her milk we are nourished;
by her spirit we are animated.

Cyprian, 200?-258, North Africa

Now I appeal to you, brothers and sisters, by the name of our
Lord Jesus Christ, that all of you be in agreement and that there be
no divisions among you, but that you be united in the same mind
and the same purpose.

1 Corinthians 1:10

A local church is a community of true believers under the
Lordship of Christ. It is the redemptive fellowship in which the
Word of God is preached by persons divinely called, and the
Sacraments are duly administered according to Christ's own
appointment. Under the discipline of the Holy Spirit the Church
exists for the maintenance of worship, the edification of believers,
and the redemption of the world.

The Book of Discipline of The United Methodist Church, 1992

Usually discussion about the Christian life begins by talking about people as individuals and later looks at how these individuals interact. Thus, we assume that life in Christ begins with the conversion of particular people, who then voluntarily assemble themselves into an organization (the church) for reasons of practical efficiency and mutual support. But we will not understand the true nature of the Christian faith so long as we assume that the church is essentially an expendable society of like-minded individuals who decide to gather together to pursue common religious concerns.

The church is, instead, a community called into being at God's initiative. It is an essential assembly, without which those who come forth from the font are still-born. To those who have been reared on a doctrine of rugged individualism, such a statement may appear to be extreme; but its truth can be demonstrated.

Without the community of Israel, which produced prophets and teachers, Scripture and liturgy, there could have been no New Testament church. Without the church, not one of us would be alive in Christ today; for our faith is dependent upon Scripture and tradition. . . .The church is God's creation and gift; it is within the church that we discover who we are in relation to God and one another.

Laurence Hull Stookey, United States

By the word of His power He gathered us out of all lands, from one end of the earth to the other end of the world, and made resurrection of our minds, and remission of our sins, and taught us that we are members one of another.

attributed to Anthony of Egypt, 250?-356?

The Church of Christ, in every age
  beset by change but Spirit-led,
must claim and test its heritage
  and keep on rising from the dead.

Fred Pratt Green, England

Christ has organized the Church from within once and for all. As a human society it is regenerated and lasts through the centuries because Christ constantly creates it and organizes it from within as his own mystical body. And this takes place because of us, because of what Christ carries out within us. Thus Christ creates us and we create him, that is, the Church.

Pope John Paul II, Poland

We do not want, as the newspapers say, a Church that will move with the world. We want a Church that will move the world.

G. K. Chesterton, 1874-1936, England

The church is in a good state when it has no other support than God.

Blaise Pascal, 1623-1662, France

CALLING TO
BAPTISM:

Professing
and Praying
with the
Church

In [Boston], the ladies who were connected with the several Christian denominations, were in the habit of holding a monthly union prayer-meeting together; and as this brought the different denominations into closer contact with each other, it caused a rich intercourse of sanctified gifts and graces amongst them, for the edification of the general body; it also greatly promoted Christian love, for the pure, genial currents supplied by genuine gospel faith, purified the disciples from party bigotry, and caused them to love one another for the truth's sake. It was delightful indeed to hear Episcopalians, Presbyterians, Baptists, and Methodists, avow the rich enjoyments they had in the spirit of adoption from God, who gave forth the corroborating testimony of His divine witness with their spirits to their heavenly filiations. The Christian church should manifest one fold and one shepherd; one body and spirit; one hope, one Lord, one faith, one baptism; and one God and father of all who is above all, and through all, and in all (Ephesians 4:4-6).

Zilpah Elaw, 1790?-?, United States

Almighty and eternal God,
you keep together those you have united.
Look kindly on all who follow Jesus your Son.
We are all consecrated to you by our common baptism;
make us one in the fullness of faith
and keep us one in the fellowship of love.

We ask this through our Lord Jesus Christ, your Son,
who lives and reigns with you and the Holy Spirit,
one God, for ever and ever.

Prayer for Christian Unity, *The Sacramentary of the Roman Catholic Church*

Our identity is dependent on having a story that tells us who we are. Our understanding of life's meaning and purpose is dependent on having a story that tells us what the world is like and where we are going. To be a community of faith we must be a people with a story, a common memory and vision, common rituals and symbols expressive of our community's memory and vision and a common life together that manifests our community's memory and vision. The church is a story-formed community.

John Westerhoff, United States

You and I are doing wrong to the world when we do not drink in the full spirit of joy that is in the Christian Church, because it is that spirit which gives us power.

Matthew Simpson, 1811-1884, United States

United Methodists share a common heritage with Christians of every age and nation. This heritage is grounded in the apostolic witness to Jesus Christ as Savior and Lord, which is the source and measure of all valid Christian teaching.

The Book of Discipline of The United Methodist Church, 1992

The Christian is saved not in isolation but as a member of the community; he is saved in and through others. We can only be saved when praying for the salvation of all and with the aid of the prayers of all.

Timothy Ware, England

I am the church! You are the church!
We are the church together!
All who follow Jesus, all around the world!
Yes, we're the church together!

The church is not a building,
the church is not a steeple,
the church is not a resting place,
the church is a people.

Richard K. Avery and Donald Marsh, United States

Grace was in Christ . . . not simply as an individual human being, but as in the Head of the whole Church, to whom all are united as members to the head, forming a single mystic person. In consequence, the merit of Christ extends to others in so far as they are his members. In somewhat similar fashion in individual human beings the action of the head belongs in some measure to all their bodily members.

Thomas Aquinas, 1227?-1274? Europe

The sharing we do in the church, the body of Christ, is more than fellowship, more than working side by side. We share in a profound communion at the root of our beings, on levels only dimly accessible to consciousness. We are lives interconnected at the core. Flowing from the same spring, the waters of divine life pulse through each of our beings, joining us as tributaries angling off from a single waterway.

We are mothers to one another, carrying each other beneath our hearts, slinging one another high on waiting hips when the walking becomes too difficult, lifting our hands behind each others necks to bring hungry mouths to feed, giving our own substance to bring each other life.

Wendy Wright, United States

The Church is like a great ship being pounded by the waves of life's different stresses. Our duty is not to abandon ship, but to keep her on her course.

Julius Pomerius, fifth century, North Africa/ France

CALLING TO
BAPTISM:

Professing
and Praying
with the
Church

THE COMMUNION OF SAINTS,

Who can count the dust of Jacob,
or number the dust-cloud of Israel?
Let me die the death of the upright, and let my end be like his!

Numbers 23:10

I think the saints have been the most ambitious people,
Those who have wanted to be truly great,
and they are the only truly great persons.
Earthly heroism cannot attain the heights of a saint.
That is what I ambition for you and for me:
to be great,
ambitiously great,
because we are God's images
and we cannot be content with mediocre greatness.

Oscar Romero, 1917-1980, El Salvador

What life have you if you have not life together?
There is no life that is not lived in community.
And no community not lived in praise of God.

T.S. Eliot, 1888-1965, England

Do all you can to love everyone. If you are not yet able to, at the very least don't hate anyone. Yet you won't even manage this if you have not reached detachment from the things of this world.

You must love everyone with all your soul, hoping, however, only in God and honouring him with all your heart.

Christ's friends are not loved by all, but they sincerely love all. The friends of this world are not loved by all, but neither do they love all.

Christ's friends persevere in their love right to the end. The friends of this world persevere only so long as they do not find themselves in disagreement over worldly matters.

A faithful friend is an effective protector. When things are going well, he gives you good advice and shows you his sympathy in practical ways. When things are going badly, he defends you unselfishly and he is a deeply committed ally.

Many people have said many things about love. But if you are looking for it, you will only find it in the followers of Christ. Only they have true Love as their teacher in love.

This is the Love about which it is written: "If I have prophetic powers, and understand all mysteries and all knowledge, but have not love, I am nothing." (I Corinthians 13:2)

Whoever has love has God, because God is Love. (I John 4:16)

Maximus the Confessor, 580?-662, Asia Minor

Heaven is not only about the future, but it is also about the past and the present. It is a means of connecting Christians now alive with all who went before them. Whatever else eternal life is, it is "the communion of saints"—the bond of grace between all Christians living and dead. The loss of the concept of heaven is also the loss of a companionship we rightly feel with all who have preceded us in the faith.

Laurence Hull Stookey, United States

For all the saints, who from their labors rest,
who thee, by faith before the world confessed,
thy name, O Jesus, be forever blest. Alleluia, Alleluia!

William W. How, 1823-1897, England

Imagine a circle marked out on the ground. Suppose that this circle is the world, and that the center of the circle is God. Leading from the edge of the circle to its center are a number of lines, and these represent the paths or ways of life that people can follow. In their desire to draw near to God, the saints advance along these lines toward the middle of the circle, so that the further they go, the nearer they approach to one another as well as to God. The closer they come to God, the closer they come to one another; and the closer they come to each other, the closer they come to God . . . Such is the nature of love: the nearer we draw to God in love, the more we are united together by love for our neighbor; and the greater our union with our neighbor, the greater is our union with God.

Dorotheus of Gaza, sixth century

Receive the Word of God.
Learn its stories and study its words.
Its stories belong to us all,
    and these words speak to us all.
They tell us who we are.
They tell us that we belong to one another,
    for we are the people of God.

An Order for the Presentation of Bibles to Children

Baptism also gives us a vision of a new social order. All of us come to baptism as sinners equally guilty before God, and all of us come away from baptism as those who have been made God's adopted sons and daughters through grace. Once we grasp this, any supposed superiority based on race, social class, gender, or nationality is exposed as a lie.

Laurence Hull Stookey, United States

All praise to our redeeming Lord, who joins us by his grace, and bids us, each to each restored, together seek his face.

Charles Wesley, 1707-1788, England

CALLING TO
BAPTISM:

Professing
and Praying
with the
Church

O Lord, whose holy saints and martyrs in all times and places have endured affliction, suffering and tribulation, by the power of the Holy Cross, the armour of salvation: so likewise, we pray, send your Holy Spirit, the Comforter and Advocate of all Christians, to sustain these churches in their martyrdom, witness and mission. The world without provocation hates your Church, but you have taught us not to despair. Therefore, you who are a God at hand and not a God afar off, grant to these Christians the power to lift up their hands, their eyes and their hearts to continue their living witness in unity with the universal Church, to the glory of your most holy name.

a prayer of a contemporary Christian from Romania

God our Father, source of all holiness
the work of your hands is manifest in your saints,
the beauty of your truth is reflected in their faith.
May we who aspire to have part in their joy be filled with the
Spirit that blessed their lives,
so that having shared their faith on earth we may also know their
peace in your kingdom.
Grant this through Christ our Lord.

The Sacramentary of the Roman Catholic Church

I sing a song of the saints of God,
    patient and brave and true,
who toiled and fought and lived and died
    for the Lord they loved and knew.
And one was a doctor, and one was a queen,
    and one was a shepherdess on the green;
they were all of them saints of God,
    and I mean, God helping, to be one too.

Lesbia Scott, 1898-1986, England

Saints never know they're saints. That's why they are saints. They are too busy talking to God to look in the mirror. The same moles and wrinkles are there, but contact with the Eternal has given them a borrowed glory. Divine conversation has left a residual luster. The saints are not conscious that they are different, but the dark world is quite aware of the light which has invaded it. The world does not need to ask "Have you talked with God?" but only, "What did He say?"

Wilbur E. Rees, United States

Bring me to see, Lord, bring me yet to see
  Those nations of thy glory and thy grace
  Who splendid in thy splendour worship Thee.
Light in all my eyes, content in every face,
  Raptures and voices one while manifold,
  Love and are well-beloved the ransomed race:—
Great mitred priests, great kings in crowns of gold,
  Patriarchs who head the army of their sons,
  Matrons and mothers by their own extolled,
Wise and most harmless holy little ones,
  Virgins who, making merry, lead the dance,
  Full-breathed victorious racers from all runs,
Home-comers out of every change and chance,
  Hermits restored to social neighbourhood,
  Aspects which reproduce One Countenance,
Life-losers with their losses all made good,
  All blessed hungry and athirst sufficed,
  All who bore crosses round the Holy Rood,
Friends, brethren, sisters, of Lord Jesus Christ.

Christina Rossetti, 1830–1894, England

The Saints were so completely dead to themselves that they cared very little whether others agreed with them or not.

attributed to John Vianney, 1786–1859, France

I remembered a Sunday school teacher who welcomed me to her first-grade Vacation Bible School class. I can still taste her Ritz crackers and cherry Kool-Aid. I can remember the way she stuck pictures of Jesus on a flannelgraph board. She let me know that the church was a place where I was loved.

I remember a car salesman who tried to teach a Sunday school class of seventh-grade boys, most of the time with minimal success! I don't remember much of what he taught us, but I do remember that we were very difficult to teach. By God's grace, I believe he forgave us. And by God's grace, he was there every week, and we knew he cared.

I remember a retired Methodist preacher who sat on the end of the second pew in my home church. When we came into the sanctuary, we'd find him already sitting there, his head bowed down on the pew in front of him in prayer. I can still hear his voice and feel his bony hand on mine when he prayed, before I went off to college, that I'd become a Methodist preacher.

I am who I am today because of the communion of saints, because of ordinary folks through whom I experienced the love of God. I believe in this affirmation, which hurls us out into the infinity of eternal life, because I have experienced it right here on earth. And I've experienced it here, with you. Every time I look out at this congregation I feel like the person who was lucky enough to be playing the tuba when it started raining silver dollars. Right here, right now, this is the communion of saints.

James A. Harnish, United States

CALLING TO
BAPTISM:

Professing
and Praying
with the
Church

THE FORGIVENESS OF SINS,

What merit, then, has man before grace which could make it possible for him to receive grace, when nothing but grace produces good merit in us; and what else but his gifts does God crown when he crowns our merits?

Augustine, 354-430, North Africa

O Lord God,
   the watchers of Zion have called peace, peace,
   when there was no peace.
Wherefore have you so long withheld from us
   the influence of your Holy Spirit?
Why have you hardened our hearts?
It is because we have honored you with our lips,
   when our hearts were far from you.

Return again to us, O Lord God,
   and pardon this iniquity of your servants.
Cause your face to shine upon us, and we shall be saved.
O visit us with your salvation.
Raise up sons and daughters from Abraham and Sarah,
   and grant that there might come
      a mighty shaking of dry bones among us,
and a great ingathering of souls.

Be pleased to grant
   that the kingdom of our Lord Jesus Christ may be built up;
that all nations and kindreds and tongues and peoples
   might be brought to the knowledge of the truth,
and we at last meet around your throne,
   and join in celebrating your praises. Amen.

Maria Stewart, 1803-1879, United States

Hear the good news:
   Christ died for us while we were yet sinners;
   that proves God's love toward us.
In the name of Jesus Christ, you are forgiven!

Confession and Pardon, Service of Word and Table

What happened to us in baptism is bestowed upon us anew in confession [of sin]. We are delivered out of darkness into the kingdom of Jesus Christ. That is joyful news. Confession is the renewal of the joy of baptism. "Weeping may endure for a night, but joy cometh in the morning" (Psalm 30:5).

Dietrich Bonhoeffer, 1906-1945, Germany

The word "redemption" sounds old-fashioned and meaningless to many people. It means literally to be "bought back," and came into use originally from the idea that a person who had become a slave to sin could be restored to freedom only when a price was paid. In spite of the outmoded metaphor, there is a deep meaning here, for the Christian believes that Jesus in love for men did something for us which we could not do for ourselves. However, we shall understand it better if we change the word a little and say that Christ has "brought" us back to God. Redemption means salvation, and salvation means healing, health, wholeness of living. To say that "Jesus saves" is to say that when we have strayed from our true home in God, when our souls are sick and at loose ends, he brings us back and heals and unifies us for strong and victorious living.

Georgia Harkness, 1891-1974, United States

How can we sinners know our sins on earth forgiven?
How can my gracious Savior show my name inscribed in heaven?

What we have felt and seen, with confidence we tell,
and publish to the ends of earth the signs infallible.

We who in Christ believe that he for us hath died,
we all his unknown peace receive and feel his blood applied.

We by his Spirit prove and know the things of God,
the things which freely of his love he hath on us bestowed.

The meek and lowly heart that in our Savior was,
to us that Spirit doth impart and signs us with his cross.

Our nature's turned, our mind transformed in all its powers,
and both the witnesses are joined, the Spirit of God with ours.

Charles Wesley, 1707-1788, England

In the evening I went very unwillingly to a society in Aldersgate Street, where one was reading Luther's preface to the Epistle to the Romans. About a quarter before nine, while he was describing the change which God works in the heart through faith in Christ, I felt my heart strangely warmed. I felt I did trust in Christ, Christ alone, for salvation; and an assurance was given me that he had taken away my sins, even mine, and saved me from the law of sin and death.

John Wesley, 1703-1791, England

If we confess our sins, he who is faithful and just will forgive us our sins and cleanse us from all unrighteousness.

1 John 1:9

73

CALLING TO
BAPTISM:

Professing
and Praying
with the
Church

God of all nations, we praise you that in Christ
the barriers that have separated humanity are torn down.
Yet we confess our slowness to open our hearts and minds
to those of other lands, tongues, and races.
Deliver us from the sins of fear and prejudice,
that we may move toward the day
when all are one in Jesus Christ. Amen.

Ruth Duck, United States

Have mercy on me, O God,
according to your steadfast love;
according to your abundant mercy
blot out my transgressions.
Wash me thoroughly from my iniquity,
and cleanse me from my sin. . . .
Create in me a clean heart, O God,
and put a new and right spirit within me.
Do not cast me away from your presence,
and do not take your holy spirit from me.
Restore to me the joy of your salvation,
and sustain in me a willing spirit.

Psalm 51:1-2, 10-12

Augustine said:
"It is by running along the road of true love that we can reach
our heavenly homeland.
"Without love, everything we do is useless. We are wasting
our energies if we do not have love, which is God.
"Human beings only become perfect when they are overflow-
ing with love.
"One can believe in the right way, but without love one can-
not attain eternal happiness.
"Love is so strong that without it neither prophecy nor martyr-
dom avail.
"Love is the sweet and saving food without which the rich are
poor, thanks to which the poor become rich.
"Enlarge your love to the size of the world if you want to love
Christ, since the members of Christ are to be found all over the world.
"Only those who have the perfection of Christ's love are able
to live together. Those who are without it continually upset one
another and their anxiety is a misery to others."

Defensor Grammaticus, seventh century, France

Gracious Voices

I'm sure glad you can erase the tape, Lord. I don't think I could
stand hearing it played back. You push the button, and there is
only silence. How graciously you destroy the past! That's what hell
is, isn't it? Having the tape played back?

Wilbur E. Rees, United States

Christians do not believe *in* sin, do not believe this or that *about* sin. Instead we rely on the *forgiveness* of sins. What we rely on is therefore not a dead and deadly law but a life-giving word and deed. The talk of forgiveness of sins does not leave us alone with our uneasy or easy consciences but places us in community with "the holy catholic church." It does not lead us into dis-spirited pre-occupation with guilt but into the freedom and joy that comes from the Holy Spirit. It does not turn us inward upon ourselves but turns us in hope and longing toward the transformation of heaven and earth, the dawning of the reign of God.

Theodore Jennings, United States

Jesus said to them again, "Peace be with you. As the Father has sent me, so I send you." When he had said this, he breathed on them and said to them, "Receive the Holy Spirit. If you forgive the sins of any, they are forgiven them; if you retain the sins of any, they are retained."

John 20:21–23

The Lord God is merciful and gracious,
  endlessly patient, loving, and true,
  showing mercy to thousands,
  forgiving iniquity, transgression,
  and sin, and granting pardon.

Gates of Prayer: The New Union Prayerbook

THE RESURRECTION OF THE BODY
AND THE LIFE EVERLASTING. AMEN.

Beloved, we are God's children now; what we will be has not yet been revealed. What we do know is this: when he is revealed, we will be like him, for we will see him as he is.

1 John 3:2

We believe also in the resurrection of the dead. For there will be, in truth there will be, a resurrection of the dead, and by resurrection we mean resurrection of bodies. For resurrection is the second state of that which has fallen. For the souls are immortal, and hence how can they rise again? . . . It is, then, this very body, which is corruptible and liable to dissolution, that will rise again incorruptible.

John of Damascus, 675?–749

If you, O Lord, should mark iniquities, Lord, who could stand? But there is forgiveness with you, so that you may be revered.

Psalm 130:3–4

CALLING TO
BAPTISM:

Professing
and Praying
with the
Church

As for paradise, God has placed no doors there.
Whoever wishes to enter, does so.
All-merciful God stands there with His arms open
waiting to receive us into His glory.
I also see, however,
That the divine essence is so pure and light-filled
—much more than we can imagine—
That the soul that has but the slightest imperfection
would rather throw itself into a thousand hells
than appear before the divine presence.

Catherine of Genoa, 1447-1510, Italy

Swing low, sweet chariot, coming for to carry me home;
swing low, sweet chariot, coming for to carry me home.
If you get up there before I do, coming for to carry me home;
tell all my friends I'm coming too, coming for to carry me home.

African-American spiritual

How speak trans-human change to human sense?
  Let the example speak until God's grace
  grants the pure spirit the experience.
Whether I rose in only the last created
  part of my being [the soul], O Love that rulest Heaven
  Thou knowest, by whose lamp I was translated.
When the Great Wheel that spins eternally
  in longing for Thee, captured my attention
  by that harmony attuned and heard by Thee,
I saw ablaze with sun from side to side
  a reach of Heaven: not all the rains and rivers
  of all of time could make a sea so wide.
That radiance and that new-heard melody
  fired me with such a yearning for their Cause
  as I had never felt before.

Dante Alighieri, 1265-1321, Italy

Before us it is blessed, behind us it is blessed,
  below us it is blessed, above us it is blessed,
  around us it is blessed as we set out with Christ.
Our speech is blessed as we set out for God.
With beauty before us, with beauty behind us,
  with beauty below us, with beauty above us,
  with beauty around us, we set out for a holy place indeed.
  Amen.

traditional Navaho prayer

Gracious Voices

The Christians included a strange declaration in their Creed. They said they believed in and wished for the resurrection of the body. As if the body were the only thing of any importance.

But could there be anything more important? Could there be anything more beautiful?

It is like a garden, where flowers and fruits grow.

The smile grows there,
generosity,
compassion,
the will to struggle,
hope;
the desire to plant gardens,
to bear children,
to hold hands and stroll,
to know. . . .

And its ever-rising waters overflow, they run out of it, and the dry desert becomes a watered oasis. That's the way it is: in this body, so small, so ephemeral, a whole universe lives, and if it could, it would surely give its life for the life of the world. God's desire is revealed in our body. After all, what the doctrine of the incarnation whispers to us is that God, eternally, wants a body like ours. Have you ever thought about this? that at Christmas what is celebrated is our body, as something that God desires?

But the body is not an overflowing spring: it is a welcoming lap.

The ear that hears the lament, in silence, without anything said.

The hand that grasps another.

The poem, which is the magic that transforms the world, putting in it invisible things, revealed only by the word.

The magical capacity to hear someone's tears, far away, never seen, and to weep also.

My body overflows and fertilizes the world.

The world overflows, and my body receives it.

So simple, so lovely.

Rubem Alves, Brazil

I have been made for Heaven and Heaven for me.

attributed to Joseph Cafasso, 1811–1860, Italy

CALLING TO
BAPTISM:

Professing
and Praying
with the
Church

Although the mystery of death utterly beggars the imagination, the Church has been taught by divine revelation and firmly teaches that the human person has been created by God for a blissful purpose beyond the reach of earthly misery. In addition, that bodily death from which people would have been immune had they not sinned will be vanquished according to the Christian faith, when those who were ruined by their own doing are restored to wholeness by an almighty and merciful Savior.

Vatican Council II, 1962-1965

Will He not give us all things when we are with Him? What shall our life and our nature not be when His promise unto us shall have been fulfilled! What will the spirit of man be like when it is placed above every vice that masters and subdues—when, its warfare ended, it is wholly at peace?

Augustine, 354-430, North Africa

It is not said, "May the joy of thy Lord enter into thee," but "Enter thou into the joy of thy Lord," which is a proof that the joy will be greater than we can conceive. We shall enter into a great sea of divine and eternal joy, which will fill us within and without, and surround us on all sides.

attributed to Robert Bellarmine, 1542-1621, Italy

Heaven is not divided by the number of those who reign, nor lessened by being shared, nor disturbed by its multitude, nor disordered by its inequality of ranks, nor changed by motion, nor measured by time.

attributed to Bonaventure, 1221-1274, Italy

Now listen to something astounding. How wondrous to be within and without, to grasp and to be embraced, to see and to be what is seen, to hold and to be held: This is the final end where the spirit remains at rest in the unity of blissful eternity.

Meister Eckhart, 1260?-1327, Germany

Suppose the ocean to be so enlarged as to include all the space between the earth and the starry heavens. Suppose a drop of this water to be annihilated once in a thousand years; yet that whole space of duration wherein this ocean would be annihilating, at the rate of one drop in a thousand years, would be infinitely less in proportion to eternity than one drop of water to that whole ocean.

John Wesley, 1703-1791, England

Gracious Voices

I remember one night at the dinner table when two college students asked, rather condescendingly, if I needed God in order to be happy (blessed). And I said, "Yes. I do. I cannot do it on my own." Simply acknowledging my lack of ability to be in control of the vast technological complex in which my life is set helps free me from its steel net.

Okay, they agreed. So we know we can't control traffic jams and sanitation-department strikes and flu epidemics, but certainly you can't believe in heaven, can you? All that pie-in-the-sky stuff?

Certainly not pie-in-the-sky. Whoever dreamed that one up didn't have much imagination. But the Beatitudes tell me that Blessed are the poor in spirit: for theirs is the kingdom of heaven. That's the very first one. I may hold off on heaven till the last of the Beatitudes because its going to take a steady look at all of them to get me ready. All I know for now is that wherever God is, heaven is, and if I don't have glimpses of it here and now, I'm not going to know it anywhere else.

Madeleine L'Engle, United States

You are dust, and to dust you shall return.

Genesis 3:19

Everyman: What desireth God of me?

Death: That shall I show thee:
A reckoning he will needs have
Without any longer respite.

Everyman: To give a reckoning longer leisure I crave.
This blind matter troubleth my wit.

Everyman, Medieval play

Oh! what a beautiful city,
Oh! what a beautiful city,
Oh! what a beautiful city,
Twelve gates to the city, Hallelu!

Three gates to the east!
Three gates to the west!
Three gates to the north!
Three gates to the south!
Twelve gates to the city, Hallelu!

African-American spiritual

God must, in some way or other, make room, hollowing us out and emptying us, if God is finally to penetrate into us. And in order to assimilate us, God must break the molecules of our being so as to re-cast and re-model us. The function of death is to provide the necessary entrance into our inmost selves.

Pierre Teilhard de Chardin, 1881-1955, France

CALLING TO
BAPTISM:

Professing
and Praying
with the
Church

Absolute peace and tranquility will reign everywhere by divine order. When all is finished, the elements, as you see, will sparkle with a peerless brightness and beauty, all traces of grime and filth having disappeared. For fire will shine without burning, like the dawn, the air will glitter in complete transparency, the waters will be limpid and calm, without flooding or devastating the land, and the earth will appear strong and even, without fragility or defects. There will be calm and beauty everywhere.

Hildegard of Bingen, 1098-1179, Germany

In anticipation of this eternal glory, God will sometimes inflame the senses of his devout friends with unspeakable delight and consolation even here in this life. And not just once or twice, but perhaps very often as he judges best. This delight, however, does not originate outside the person, entering through the windows of the faculties, but wells up from an excess of joy and true devotion of spirit.

Anonymous, The Cloud of Unknowing, fourteenth century, England

This world is not conclusion;
  A sequel stands beyond,
Invisible, as music,
  But positive, as sound.
It beckons and it baffles;
  Philosophies don't know,
And through a riddle, at the last,
  Sagacity must go.
To guess it puzzles scholars;
  To gain it, men have shown
Contempt of generations
  And crucifixion known.

Emily Dickinson, 1830-1886, United States

Death, be not proud, though some have called thee
Mighty and dreadful, for thou art not so;
For those whom thou think'st thou dost overthrow
Die not, poor Death, nor yet canst thou kill me.

John Donne, 1573-1631, England

Steal away, steal away;
steal away to Jesus.
Steal away, steal away home.
I ain't got long to stay here.
My Lord he calls me,
he calls me by the thunder;
the trumpet sounds within-a my soul.
I ain't got long to stay here.

African-American spiritual

Gracious Voices

THE LORD'S PRAYER

Our Father in heaven,
  hallowed be your name,
  your kingdom come,
  your will be done, on earth as in heaven.
Give us today our daily bread.
Forgive us our sins
  as we forgive those who sin against us.
Save us from the time of trial
  and deliver us from evil.
For the kingdom, the power, and the glory are yours
  now and for ever. Amen.

OUR FATHER IN HEAVEN,

Say, "Abba. Pop. Poppa. Dadee," Jesus told them. They must have been confused at the time. God heretofore had been farther away than that. God is God and a human is human. Now God and we are kinfolks.

Will Campbell, United States

God, Who stands so decisively over against our life, the Source of all splendour and all joy, is yet in closest and most cherishing contact with us; and draws us, beyond all splendour and joy, into Truth. He has created in us such a craving for Himself alone, that even the brief flashes of Eternity which sometimes visit us make all else seem dust and ashes, lifeless and unreal. Hence there should be no situation in our life, no attitude, no pre-occupation or relationship, from which we cannot look up to this God of absolute Truth and say, "Our Father," of ourselves and of all other souls involved. We recognize him, says St. John of the Cross, because we already carry in our hearts a rough sketch of the beloved countenance. Looking into these deeps, as into a quiet pool in the dark forest, we there find looking back at us the Face we implicitly long for and already know. It is set in another world, another light: yet it is here. As we realize this, our prayer widens until it embraces the extremes of awestruck adoration and confident love, and fuses them in one.

Evelyn Underhill, 1875-1941, England

For me, prayer means launching out of the heart towards God; it means lifting up one's eyes, quite simply, to Heaven, a cry of grateful love from the crest of joy or the trough of despair; it's a vast, supernatural force which opens out my heart, and binds me close to Jesus.

Thérèse de Lisieux, 1873-1897, France

I repeat: to know how to say the Our Father, and to know how to put it into practice, this is the perfection of the Christian life.

Pope John XXIII, 1881-1963, Italy

CALLING TO
BAPTISM:

Professing
and Praying
with the
Church

The care the eagle gives her young,
safe in her lofty nest,
is like the tender love of God for us made manifest.

And if we flutter helplessly, as fledgling eagles fall,
beneath us lift God's mighty wings to bear us,
one and all.

R. Deane Postlethwaite, United States

I have always been fascinated by the fact that Jesus gave the Lord's Prayer in response to the request "Lord, teach us to pray." Here is the open admission on the part of the disciples that they did not know how to pray, or at least that they could stand some improvement in their prayer life. Jesus accepted this request at face value and went on from there. Every time a person expresses embarrassment at his or her prayer life—or the lack of it—I derive great joy from telling the person that he or she has just perfectly fulfilled the qualifications for becoming a praying person.

Steve Harper, United States

We may observe, in general, concerning this divine prayer, First, that it contains all we can reasonably and innocently pray for. There is nothing which we have need to ask of God, nothing which we can ask without offending him, which is not included, either directly or indirectly, in this comprehensive form. Secondly, that it contains all we can reasonably or innocently desire; whatever is for the glory of God, whatever is needful or profitable, not only for ourselves, but for every creature in heaven and earth. And, indeed, our prayers are the proper test of our desires; nothing being fit to have a place in our desires which is not fit to have a place in our prayers: What we may not pray for, neither should we desire. Thirdly, that it contains all our duty to God and man; whatsoever things are pure and holy, whatsoever God requires of the children of men, whatsoever is acceptable in his sight, whatsoever it is whereby we may profit our neighbor, being expressed or implied therein.

John Wesley, 1703-1791, England

I do not always feel like a child of God. I do not always look like a child of God. God knows I do not always act like a child of God! But I am. I am one of God's children not because of what I did or because of who I am but because God chose me, out of all the universe, to be his child. I am owned. When I am anxious or alone or defeated, baptism ought to speak a firm word of comfort to me: "Relax, be calm. You did not choose me, I chose you."

William Willimon, United States

Gracious Voices

In prayer one drinks the wine that gladdens a man's heart, the intoxicating wine of the Spirit that drowns all memory of the pleasures of the flesh. It drenches anew the arid recesses of the conscience, stimulates digestion of the meats of good works, fills the faculties of the soul with a robust faith, a solid hope, a love which is living and true. It enriches all the actions of our life.

Bernard of Clairvaux, 1090-1153, France

On what basis is it possible to bridge the gulf between the absence of God and the promise of God? There is no point in denying that this chasm exists. To deny it is to render prayer impossible and to make a mockery of God's promise. We make a mockery of God's promise when we make it conform to "the way things are," when we settle for less than God. It is but a short step—if it is any step at all—from this resignation to blasphemous idolatry. If we settle for less than God, we are likely to make that "less" into God, and thus "God" becomes the guarantor of the way things are. This is the idolatry of those who have settled down in the land—who transform Yahweh into Baal. Under these circumstances prayer, too, ceases. Instead of asking God to be God, and thus to transform earth and heaven, we ask that heaven ratify earth.

Theodore Jennings, United States

I don't say anything to God. I just sit and look at him and let him look at me.

attributed to villager of Ars, nineteenth century, France

Our Father. Not mine only who now cry to him, but ours in the most extensive sense. The God and Father of the spirits of all flesh; the Father of angels and men: So the very Heathens acknowledge him to be. . . . The Father of the universe, of all the families both in heaven and earth. Therefore with him there is no respect of persons. He loves all that he has made. He is loving unto every man, and his mercy is over all his works. And the Lord's delight is in them that fear him, and put their trust in his mercy: in them that trust in him through the Son of his love, knowing they are accepted in the Beloved. But if God so loved us, we ought also to love one another; yea all mankind; seeing God so loved the world that he gave his only begotten Son, even to die the death, that they might not perish, but have everlasting life.

John Wesley, 1703-1791, England

Likewise the Spirit helps us in our weakness; for we do not know how to pray as we ought, but that very Spirit intercedes with sighs too deep for words. And God, who searches the heart, knows what is the mind of the Spirit, because the Spirit intercedes for the saints according to the will of God.

Romans 8:26-27

CALLING TO
BAPTISM:

Professing
and Praying
with the
Church

Regarding "Who art in heaven": These words I think have a very deep meaning. They remind us of the homeland we have abandoned, of the citizenship we have lost.

In the parable of the young man who left his father's house, went off the rails and was reduced to living with pigs, the Word of God shows us human wretchedness.

That young man did not find his one-time happiness again until he had realized his moral degradation, had looked into his own heart and had pronounced the words of confession.

These words almost agree with the Lord's prayer, because the prodigal son says: "Father, I have sinned against heaven and against you." (Luke 15:21)

He would not confess himself to be a sinner against heaven if he were not convinced that the homeland he had left at the time of his going astray were not in actual fact heaven.

By this confession of his he makes himself worthy once again to stand in the presence of his father who runs toward him, embraces him, and kisses him.

The conclusion is this. To return to heaven there is only one route and that is to admit one's sinfulness and seek to avoid it. To make the decision to avoid it is already to be perfecting one's likeness to God.

Gregory of Nyssa, 331?-394, Asia Minor

Give us, Señor, a little sun, a little happiness, and some work.
Give us a heart to comfort those in pain.
Give us the ability to be good, strong, wise, and free,
   so that we may be as generous with others as we are with ourselves.
Finally, Señor, let us all live as your own one family. Amen.

from a church wall in Mexico, twentieth century

HALLOWED BE YOUR NAME,

Bless the LORD, O my soul,
   and all that is within me,
   bless his holy name.
Bless the LORD, O my soul,
   and do not forget all his benefits—
who forgives all your iniquity,
   who heals all your diseases,
who redeems your life from the Pit,
   who crowns you with steadfast love and mercy,
who satisfies you with good as long as you live
   so that your youth is renewed like the eagle's.

Psalm 103:1-5

My words fly up, my thoughts remain below.
Words without thoughts never to heaven go.

William Shakespeare, 1564-1616, England

What is the meaning of the words "name" and "hallow"?

"Name" denotes the proper and exclusive nature of the being that carries it and indicates the general effect of its qualities. In human beings these qualities can change, and with them their names too. Abram came to be called Abraham, Simon became Peter, and Saul's name was changed to Paul. By contrast in the case of God who is immutable, who never changes, there is but one name, the "I am" that was given him in Exodus. (Exodus 3:14) We all endeavor to reflect on God to understand his nature, but they are few indeed that succeed in sensing his holiness.

Jesus' prayer teaches us that God is holy. It helps us to discover the holiness of the Being that creates, provides, judges, chooses and abounds in generosity, welcomes and rejects, rewards and punishes equally. This is what characterizes the quality that belongs to God, the quality that the Scriptures call by the name of God.

Therefore in the Scriptures we read: "You shall not take the name of the Lord your God in vain," (Exodus 20:7) and again: "May my teaching drop as the rain, my speech distill as the dew, as the gentle rain upon the tender grass, and as the showers upon the herb, for I will proclaim the name of the Lord." (Deuteronomy 32:2)

Anyone who prays ought therefore to ask that the name of God may be hallowed, as is said also in the Psalms: "Let us exalt his name together." (Psalm 34:3) The Psalmist hopes that we may arrive, in harmony of spirit, at a true understanding of the nature of God.

Origen, third century, Egypt

The love of God Most High for our soul is so wonderful that it surpasses all knowledge. No created being can know the great- ness, the sweetness, the tenderness of the love that our Maker has for us. By [God's] grace and help therefore let us in spirit stand and gaze, eternally marvelling at the supreme, surpassing, singlemind- ed, incalculable love that God, who is goodness, has for us. Then we can ask reverently of our lover whatever we will.

Julian of Norwich, 1342?-?, England

Enable me, O God, to collect and compose my thoughts before an immediate approach to Thee in prayer. May I be careful to have my mind in order when I take upon myself the honor to speak to the Sovereign Lord of the Universe, remembering that upon the temper of my soul depends, in very great measure, my success.

Thou art infinitely too great to be trifled with; too wise to be imposed on by a mock devotion and dost abhor a sacrifice without a heart. Help me to entertain an habitual sense of Thy perfections, as an admirable help against cold and formal performances. Save me from engaging in rash and precipitate prayers and from abrupt breaking away to follow business or pleasure, as though I had never prayed. Amen.

Susanna Wesley, 1669-1742, England

You can't pray a lie.

Mark Twain, 1835-1910, United States

CALLING TO
BAPTISM:

Professing
and Praying
with the
Church

The feelings have their own language, in which they disclose themselves even against their will. Fear has its trembling, grief its anguished groans, love its cries of delight. . . . Do they constitute a reasoned discourse, a deliberate utterance, a pre-meditated speech? Most certainly such expressions of feeling are not produced by the processes of the mind but by spontaneous impulses. So a strong and burning love, particularly the love of God, does not stop to consider the order, the grammar, the flow, or the number of words it employs when it cannot contain itself, provided it senses it suffers no loss thereby. Sometimes it needs no words, no expression at all, being content with aspirations alone. Thus it is that the bride, aflame with holy love, doubtless seeking to quench a little the fire of the love she endures, gives no thought to her words or the manner of her speech. But, impelled by love, she does not speak clearly but bursts out with whatever comes to her lips.

Bernard of Clairvaux, 1090-1153, France

All our life is like a day of celebration for us; we are convinced, in fact, that God is always everywhere. We work while singing, we sail while reciting hymns, we accomplish all other occupations of life while praying.

Clement of Alexandria, second century, Egypt

Holy, holy, holy Lord, God of power and might,
heaven and earth are full of your glory.
    Hosanna in the highest.
Blessed is he who comes in the name of the Lord.
    Hosanna in the highest.

Great Thanksgiving, Service of Word and Table

There is no Holy One like the LORD,
    no one besides you;
    there is no Rock like our God.

1 Samuel 2:2

We can, however, be almost certain that those whose love of God has caused the disappearance of the pure loves belonging to our life here below are no true friends of God.

Our neighbor, our friends, religious ceremonies, and the beauty of the world do not fall to the level of unrealities after the soul has had direct contact with God. On the contrary, it is only then that these things become real. Previously they were half dreams. Previously they had no reality.

Simone Weil, 1909-1943, France

Gracious Voices

YOUR KINGDOM COME,

"The kingdom of God is within us," that is, on our lips and in our hearts. (Luke 17:21) Therefore anyone who prays that the kingdom of God may not delay its coming is praying that it may be consolidated, extended, and reach its fullness within him. Our Lord in fact dwells in all holy people who recognize God as their king and obey his spiritual laws. The Father is present in the perfect soul and Christ reigns together with the Father, according to his own actual word "If someone loves me . . . we will come to him and make our home with him." (John 14:23)

The kingdom will not reach its fullness in each of us until wisdom and the other virtues are perfected in us. Perfection is reached at the end of a journey, so we ought to be "forgetting what lies behind and straining forward to what lies ahead." (Philippians 3:13)

In other words, on the one hand the believer is a tireless traveller and on the other hand the kingdom of God will reach its completion in us only when the words of the Apostle are fulfilled: "When he has subjected all things, Christ will deliver up the kingdom to the Father, that God may be all in all."(1 Corinthians 15:24-28)

Let us subdue our members to produce the fruits of the Spirit. Then the Lord will walk with us as in a spiritual paradise. He alone will reign in us, together with Christ. And we shall already possess the benefits of the new birth and of the resurrection.

Origen, third century, Egypt

Blessed are the poor in spirit, for theirs is the kingdom of heaven.
Blessed are those who mourn, for they will be comforted.
Blessed are the meek, for they will inherit the earth.
Blessed are those who hunger and thirst for righteousness,
    for they will be filled.
Blessed are the merciful, for they will receive mercy.
Blessed are the pure in heart, for they will see God.
Blessed are the peacemakers, for they will be called children of God.
Blessed are those who are persecuted for righteousness' sake,
    for theirs is the kingdom of heaven.
Blessed are you when people revile you and persecute you
    and utter all kinds of evil against you falsely on my account.
Rejoice and be glad, for your reward is great in heaven, for in the
    same way they persecuted the prophets who were before you.

Matthew 5:3-12

For the kingdom of God—That is, true religion, does not consist in external observances. But in *righteousness*—The image of God stamped on the heart; the love of God and man, accompanied with the *peace* that passeth all understanding, *and joy in the Holy Ghost.*

John Wesley, 1703-1791, England

Try hard to wall up the cell of your heart, so that your enemies may not be able to get in, and decorate this cell with the virtues.

Catherine of Siena, 1347-1380, Italy

87

CALLING TO
BAPTISM:

Professing
and Praying
with the
Church

Where now are the friends, the make-believes, the followers of the fashion? Where the suppers and feasts? Where the swarms of hangers-on? The strong wine decanting all day long, the cooks and the daintily dressed table, the attendants on greatness and all the words and ways they used to please? They were all night and dreaming: now it is day and they are vanished. They were spring flowers, and, spring over, they all are faded together. They were a shadow, and it has traveled on beyond. They were smoke, and it has gone out in the air. They were bubbles and are broken. They were cobweb, and are swept away. And so this spiritual refrain is left again and again for us to sing: vanity of vanities, all is vanity.

John Chrysostom, 345?-407, West Syria

One day my mother and another colored sister waited until all the white people had, as they thought, been served, when they started for the communion table. Just as they reached the lower door, two of the poorer class of white folks arose to go to the table. At this, a mother in Israel caught hold of my mother's dress and said to her, "Don't you know better than to go to the table when white folks are there?" Ah! she did know better than to do such a thing purposely. This was one of the fruits of slavery. Although pro-fessing to love the same God, members of the same church, and expecting to find the same heaven at last, they could not partake of the Lord's Supper until the lowest of the whites had been served. Were they led by the Holy Spirit? Who shall say? The Spirit of Truth can never be mistaken, nor can he inspire anything unholy. How many at the present day profess great spirituality, and even holiness, and yet are deluded by a spirit of error, which leads them to say to the poor and colored ones among them, "Stand back a little—I am holier than thou."

Julia A. J. Foote, 1823?-1900?, United States

However, prayer is no panacea, no substitute for action. It is, rather, like a beam thrown from a flashlight before us into the dark-ness. It is in this light that we who grope, stumble, and climb, dis-cover where we stand, what surrounds us, and the course which we should choose. Prayer makes visible the right, and reveals what is hampering and false. In its radiance, we behold the worth of our efforts, the range of our hopes, and the meaning of our deeds. Envy and fear, despair and resentment, anguish and grief, which lie heavily upon the heart, are dispelled like shadows by its light.

Abraham Joshua Heschel, 1907-1972, Germany/United States

Gracious Voices

The central meaning of the Kingdom is the righteous, loving rule of God. God demands allegiance like a king; he loves us like a father. If one takes the rule of God as the keynote, many otherwise contradictory passages can be harmonized. The rule of God is already present, yet it must come in the fullness of time when men repent and seek to do God's will on earth. It comes in this world, but the final victory of God's rule lies, not on earth, but in a realm beyond this world. It grows gradually and almost imperceptibly, like leaven or mustard seed; it comes suddenly, like a thief in the night, or the bridegroom at a wedding, and one must be ready and on the watch. "It is the Father's good pleasure to give you the kingdom," yet he gives it to him who, prizing it like a pearl of great price or a treasure hid in the field, gives it for all he has.

Georgia Harkness, 1891-1974, United States

Thy kingdom come . . . This prayer does two things: it humbles us and it uplifts us.

It humbles us in that it makes us confess openly that God's kingdom has not yet come to us. The which, if it is earnestly contemplated and thoughtfully prayed, is a dreadful thing to us, and will grieve and pain every devout heart; for it follows that we are still cast out, bereft of our most beloved fatherland. These are two woeful and deplorable losses: the first, that God the Father is bereft of His kingdom in us, that He who is and should be Lord of everything, should through us alone be kept from such lofty power and honor. This must without doubt pain all who love God well and truly. The other loss is ours: that we should still be kept in misery, in foreign lands amongst such mighty foes.

Further, when such thoughts have humbled us and have made our wretchedness manifest unto us, consolation follows, and our kind Master, the Lord Christ, teaches us that we should ask and crave to be taken out of that wretchedness, and not despair; for those who confess that they themselves are hindering God's kingdom from coming, and plaintively pray that it may come, God will reward for their sufferings and prayers.

And this is why we do not pray: Let us come to Thy kingdom, as if we should run after it; but thus: Thy kingdom come to us. For the grace of God and His kingdom, with all its virtues, must come to us, if ever we are to inherit it. Of ourselves we can never come to the kingdom, just as Christ came from heaven to us who are on earth, and we did not ascend from earth into heaven, to Him.

When God reigns in us and we are His kingdom, that is blessedness.

Martin Luther, 1483-1546, Germany

When Israel was in Egypt's land, let my people go; oppressed so hard they could not stand, let my people go. Go down, Moses, way down in Egypt's land; tell old Pharoah to let my people go!

African-American spiritual

CALLING TO
BAPTISM:

Professing
and Praying
with the
Church

Lord, make me an instrument of thy peace;
where there is hatred, let me sow love;
where there is injury, pardon;
where there is doubt, faith;
where there is despair, hope;
where there is darkness, light;
and where there is sadness, joy.

O Divine Master,
grant that I may not so much seek
to be consoled as to console;
to be understood, as to understand;
to be loved, as to love;
for it is in giving that we receive;
it is in pardoning that we are pardoned,
and it is in dying that we are born to eternal life.

Francis of Assisi, 1182–1226, Italy

Once Jesus was asked by the Pharisees when the kingdom of God was coming, and he answered, "The kingdom of God is not coming with things that can be observed; nor will they say, 'Look, here it is!' or 'There it is!' For, in fact, the kingdom of God is among you."

Luke 17:20–21

Help me, Lord, to remember that religion is not to be confined to the church or closet, nor exercised only in prayer and meditation, but that everywhere I am in Thy presence. So may my every word and action have a moral content.

As defects and infirmities betray themselves in the daily accidents and common conversations of life, grant me Thy grace, O Lord, that I may watch over, regulate and govern them. Enable me so to know myself and those with whom I have to do, that I may conform to the precepts of the Gospel and train myself to those rules of wisdom and virtue of which I am capable. Help me to discern the proper season and the just occasion of every virtue, and then to apply myself to attain it, by exercising it in those beneficent activities which, for want of due reflection, may not seem of any great importance. May all the happenings of my life prove useful and beneficial to me. May all things instruct me and afford me an opportunity of exercising some virtue and daily learning and growing toward Thy likeness, let the world go which way it will. Amen.

Susanna Wesley, 1669–1742, England

Gracious Voices

O day of peace that dimly shines
  through all our hopes and dreams,
guide us to justice, truth, and love,
  delivered from our selfish schemes.
May swords of hate fall from our hands,
  our hearts from envy find release,
till by God's grace our warring world
  shall see Christ's promised reign of peace.

Then shall the wolf dwell with the lamb,
  nor shall the fierce devour the small;
as beasts and cattle calmly grace,
  a little child shall lead them all.
Then enemies shall learn to love,
  all creatures find their true accord;
the hope of peace shall be fulfilled,
  for all the earth shall know the Lord.

Carl P. Daw, United States

The kingdom of the world has become the kingdom of our Lord and of his Messiah, and he will reign forever and ever.

Revelation 11:15

The Coming of the Kingdom is perpetual. Again and again freshness, novelty, power from beyond the world, break in by unexpected paths, bringing unexpected change.

Those who cling to tradition and fear all novelty in God's relation with His world, deny the creative activity of the Holy Spirit, and forget that what is now tradition was once innovation: that the real Christian is always a revolutionary, belongs to a new race and has been given a new song. God is with the future. The supernatural virtue of Hope blesses and supports every experiment made for the glory of His Name and the good of souls: and even when violence and horror seem to overwhelm us, discerns the secret movement of the Spirit inciting to sacrifice and preparing new triumphs for the Will. In the Church, too, this process of renovation from within, this fresh invasion of Reality must constantly be repeated if she is to escape the ever-present danger of stagnation. She is not a static institution but the living Body of the living Christ—the nucleus of the Kingdom, in this world.

Evelyn Underhill, 1875-1941, England

Some people glorify biblical folk like Peter, extolling his courage, his insight, his faith, or some other alleged attribute, and telling us, "You ought to be like Peter." Be like Peter? Thickheaded? Impulsive? Cowardly? Prejudiced? God help us, we already *are* like Peter! And yet, God chooses *us,* even us, as the building blocks for his kingdom. Once again, the "hero" of the story is *God.*

William Willimon, United States

Calling to
Baptism:

Professing
and Praying
with the
Church

YOUR WILL BE DONE, ON EARTH AS IN HEAVEN.

We who are praying are still on earth ourselves. And since we reckon that all the inhabitants of heaven fulfill the will of God in heaven, it comes naturally to us to ask that we too on earth should succeed in fulfilling the divine will. That will come about, logically, if we do nothing outside that will.

When we have perfectly accomplished it, although we are still remaining on earth we shall be like the heavenly beings and will bear equally with them the image of the heavenly Being. (1Corinthians 15:49)

In the end we shall inherit the kingdom of heaven. Those who come to take our place on earth will ask that they too may become like us who are then in heaven.

In addition it is recorded that our Lord after his resurrection said to the eleven Apostles: "All authority in heaven and on earth has been given to me." (Matthew 28:18)

Jesus claimed in short to have received authority on earth equal to that which he has in heaven. The things of heaven, at the beginning, have been illuminated by the Word. And at the end of time, thanks to the authority granted to the Son of God, the things of earth will be like those of heaven which is already perfect.

So then it is clear that Christ is calling his disciples to work faithfully with him by means of their prayers. That all earthly events may come to be transformed by the authority that Christ has received both in heaven and on earth, this ought to be our prayer.

Origen, third century, Egypt

Pray that the Lord may soften the hardness of your soul.
Pray that the Lord may forgive the sins you confess to him.
Don't pray that what you want may come to pass.
It does not necessarily coincide with the will of God.
Pray rather as you have been taught, saying:
'Your will be done in me!'
Pray that the will of God may be done in everything. He, in fact, wants what is good and useful for your soul, while you are not always seeking that and only that.

Evagrius, 345?-399, Syria/Egypt

Lord, grant us, we pray thee, communion with thyself! Nothing else does satisfy us. But thou, O Christ, art even more than we have the right to ask. Thou art riches and glory and joy unspeakable. So we pray, and we trust for ourselves, that we may come into more intimate communion with thee, this day. Open our eyes to thee more and more. Give us the spirit of love and gratitude toward thee, and toward each other, and toward all the world, until our hearts shall be melted down with loving desire.

Lucy Rider Meyer, 1849-1920, United States

My ego is like a fortress.
I have built its walls stone by stone
To hold out the invasion of the love of God.

But I have stayed here long enough. There is light
Over the barriers. O my God—
The darkness of my house forgive
And overtake my soul.
I relax the barriers
I abandon all that I think I am,
All that I hope to be,
All that I believe I possess.
I let go of the past,
I withdraw my grasping hand from the future,
And in the great silence of this moment,
I alertly rest my soul.
As the sea gull lays in the wind current,
So I lay myself into the spirit of God.
My dearest human relationships,
My most precious dreams,
I surrender to His care.
All that I have called my own
I give back. All my favorite things
Which I would withhold in my storehouse
From his fearful tyranny,
I let go.
I give myself
Unto Thee, O my God. Amen.

Howard Thurman, 1900-1981, United States

When therefore we pray that the will of God may be done in earth as it is in heaven, the meaning is that all the inhabitants of the earth, even the whole race of mankind, may do the will of their Father which is in heaven, as willingly as the holy angels; that these may do it continually, even as they, without any interruption of their willing service; yes and that they may do it perfectly, that "the God of peace, through the blood of the everlasting covenant, may make them perfect in every good work to do his will, and work in them" all "which is well-pleasing in his sight."

John Wesley, 1703-1791, England

He has told you, O mortal, what is good;
    and what does the LORD require of you
but to do justice, and to love kindness,
    and to walk humbly with your God?

Micah 6:8

Wearing our straw hats and carrying our hoes, we go to our fields praising thee, O Lord. Thou art the spring wind, we are the grass. Blow thou as thou willest.

prayer from China

CALLING TO
BAPTISM:

Professing
and Praying
with the
Church

If we are not our own, but the Lord's, it is clear to what purpose all our deeds must be directed. We are not our own, therefore neither our reason nor our will should guide us in our thoughts and actions. We are not our own, therefore we should not seek what is only expedient to the flesh. We are not our own, therefore let us forget ourselves and our own interests as far as possible.

We are God's own; to him, therefore, let us live and die. We are God's own; therefore let his wisdom and his will dominate all our actions. We are God's own; therefore let every part of our existence be directed towards him as our only legitimate goal.

John Calvin, 1509-1564, France

Therefore with mind entire, faith firm, courage undaunted, love thorough, let us be ready for whatever God wills; faithfully keeping his commandments, having innocence in simplicity, peaceableness in love, modesty in lowliness, diligence in ministering, mercifulness in helping the poor, firmness in standing for truth, and sternness in keeping of discipline.

attributed to Bede the Venerable, 673?-735, England

There is, perhaps, no part of Christian experience where a greater change occurs, upon entering into this life hid with Christ in God, than in the matter of service.

In all the ordinary forms of Christian life, service is apt to have more or less of bondage in it; that is, it is done purely as a matter of duty, and often as a trial and a cross. Certain things, which at first may have been a joy and a delight, become after a while weary tasks, performed faithfully, perhaps, but with much secret disinclination, and many confessed or unconfessed wishes that they need not be done at all, or at least that they need not be done so often.

The soul finds itself saying, instead of the "May I?" of love, the "Must I?" of duty. The yoke, which was at first easy, begins to gall, and the burden feels heavy instead of light. . . .

What we need in the Christian life is to get believers to want to do God's will as much as other people *want* to do their own will. And this is the idea of the Gospel. It is what God intended for us; and it is what He promised. In describing the new covenant in Hebrews 8:6-13, He says it shall no more be the old covenant made on Sinai,—that is, a law given from the outside, controlling a man by force,—but it shall be a law written *within,* constraining us by love.

Hannah Whitall Smith, 1832-1911, United States

And indeed nothing more absurd can be imagined than wise, sublime, and heavenly prayers added to a life where neither work nor play, neither time nor money are under the direction of our prayers. If we were to see a person pretending to act wholly with regard to God in everything that this person did and yet at the same time this person never prayed—whether public or private—wouldn't we be amazed?

Yet this is the same thing as when one is very strict in devotion, being careful to observe times and places of prayer, and yet in the rest of one's life—time, labor, talents, and money—completely neglects the will of God. It is as great an absurdity to offer up holy prayers without a holy life as it is to live a holy life without prayer.

Just as we cannot live a holy life without prayer, so we cannot have prayer without a holy life. To be foolish in the way we spend our time and money is no greater a mistake than to be foolish in relation to our prayers. If our lives cannot be offered to God, how can our prayers?

William Law, 1686-1761, England

What good is it, my brothers and sisters, if you say you have faith but do not have works? Can faith save you? If a brother or sister is naked and lacks daily food, and one of you says to them, "Go in peace; keep warm and eat your fill," and yet you do not supply their bodily needs, what is the good of that? So faith by itself, if it has no works, is dead.

James 2:14-17

People say: "Yes, certainly, God has given us a free will." To this I reply: "To be sure, He has given us a *free* will; why then will you not let it remain free but make it your *own* will?" If you do with it what you will, it is not a free will. It is your own will. But God has given neither you nor any man your own will, for your own will comes from the devil and from Adam. They made the free will which they received from God into their own will. For a free will desires nothing of its own. It only cares for the will of God, and so it remains free, cleaving and clinging to nothing.

Hence you see that in this prayer God commands us to pray against ourselves, and so teaches us that we have no greater enemy than ourselves. For our will is the greatest power within us, and we must pray against it: my Father, suffer me not to have my will. Oppose my will and break it. Come what may, only let Thy will and not mine be done. For so it is in heaven; self-will is not found there. Let it be the same here on earth. Such a prayer, if it is offered, hurts our nature, for self-will is the deepest and mightiest evil in the world, and there is nothing which we love more than our own will.

Martin Luther, 1483-1546, Germany

Lord Jesus, you be the needle and I will be the cotton thread. You go through first and I will follow wherever you may lead.

prayer from the Belgian Congo

CALLING TO
BAPTISM:

Professing
and Praying
with the
Church

GIVE US TODAY OUR DAILY BREAD.

Certain monks, called "the Prayer People" because they wanted to dedicate themselves entirely to prayer, went to pay a visit to Abbot Lucius.

The aged monk asked them: "What work do you do?"

They said: "We don't do work, but we obey Paul's teaching to pray without ceasing."

The old man asked them: "Do you eat?" and they replied, "Yes." The Abbot then demanded to know who prayed instead of them while they were eating. Then he asked them: "Do you sleep?" and they replied, "Yes." The Abbot then demanded a second time to know who prayed instead of them while they were sleeping. The monks were at a loss to answer either of the two questions.

Then the old man continued: "Forgive me, but you are not doing what you say you are. I, on the other hand, succeed in working with my hands and at the same time in praying without ceasing. I start by sitting down in the presence of God. Then I begin my task of making ropes and I say: 'Have mercy on me, O God, according to your steadfast love; according to your abundant mercy blot out my transgressions.'" (Psalm 51:1)

Then he asked them if that was prayer and they replied "Yes." The old man went on: "At the end of a day passed in work and prayer, I have earned roughly sixteen shillings. Two shillings I deposit on the ground outside the door and the rest I spend on food. The person who picks up the two shillings prays in my place when I am eating or sleeping. In this way, by the grace of God, I am obedient to the teaching to pray without ceasing."

a saying of the Desert Fathers, fourth-fifth centuries, Syria/Palestine/Egypt

By "bread" we may understand all things needful, whether for our souls or bodies . . . the things pertaining to life and godliness: We understand not barely the outward bread, which our Lord terms the meat which perisheth; but much more the spiritual bread, the grace of God, the food which endures unto everlasting life. It was the judgment of many of the ancient Fathers that we are here to understand the sacramental bread also: daily received in the beginning by the whole Church of Christ, and highly esteemed, till the love of many waxed cold, as the grand channel whereby the grace of his Spirit was conveyed to the souls of all the children of God.

John Wesley, 1703-1791, England

Community is also taught in the Lord's Prayer. Christ taught us not to ask for our own bread. Not "give me my bread," but "give us our bread," that is, the communal bread. It is a false supplicator who prays, give us our bread, but then treats the bread received as his own.

Peter Walpot, 1521-1578, Austria

Bread represents life, and bread is easy to get. Moreover, nature herself gives us something to put on it to make it more tasty. The best thing to eat with bread is the peace of a good conscience. Then the bread is eaten with gusto, because it is being eaten in holiness of life.

But if you want to experience the taste of bread otherwise than in symbolic description, in the physical sense in fact, you have hunger to eat it with. Therefore, first of all, don't eat too much: you would lose your appetite for a long time. And then, let your dinner be preceded by sweat. "In the sweat of your brow you shall eat bread," is the first commandment mentioned in the Scriptures. (Genesis 3:19)

The Lord's Prayer speaks of "daily" bread. In saying that, let us remember that the life in which we ought to be interested is "daily" life. We can, each of us, only call the present time our own. Why should we worry ourselves by thinking about the future?

Our Lord tells us to pray for today, and so he prevents us from tormenting ourselves about tomorrow. It is as if he were to say to us: "He who gives you this day will also give you what you need for this day. He it is who makes the sun to rise. He it is who scatters the darkness of night and reveals to you the rays of the sun."

Gregory of Nyssa, 331?-394, Asia Minor

When I started as a traveling preacher, a single preacher was allowed to receive eighty dollars per annum, if his circuit would give it to him; but single preachers in those days seldom received over thirty or forty dollars, and often much less; and had it not been for a few presents made us by the benevolent friends of the Church, and a few dollars we made as marriage fees, we must have suffered much more than we did. But the Lord provided; and, strange as it may appear to the present generation, we got along without starving, or going naked.

Peter Cartwright, 1785-1872, United States

"Our Father, . . . Give us bread for this day." The plea is heard. There is bread for all the Father's children. A drought in Asia but a bounteous harvest in Kansas. The scorching winds of summer blow across the Midwestern plains, leaving fodder in its wake while the alluvial deltas of the southland blossom from the same warm breath. The provided bread becomes missiles and submarines. Gifts of nourishment are diverted into agents of carnage. The bread is provided. The division is of our own doing. At our peril we turn the answered petition into political gambits.

Will Campbell, United States

Give what thou dost demand, and then demand what thou wilt.

Augustine,
354-430,
North Africa

CALLING TO
BAPTISM:

Professing
and Praying
with the
Church

Abba Gregory the anchorite told us:
I was returning from Byzantium by ship and a scribe came aboard with his wife; he had to go to pray at the Holy City. The ship-master was a very devout man, given to fasting. As we sailed along, the scribe's attendants were prodigal in their use of water. When we came into the midst of the high sea, we ran out of water and we were in great distress. It was a pitiful sight: women and children and infants perishing from thirst, lying there like corpses. We were in this distressing condition for three days and abandoned hope of survival. Unable to tolerate such affliction, the scribe drew his sword, intending to kill the ship-master and the sailors. He said: "It is their fault that we are to be lost, for they did not take sufficient water on board for our needs." I interceded with the scribe, saying: "Do not do that; but rather, let us pray to our Lord Jesus Christ, our true God, who does great and wonderful things which cannot be counted (Job 34:26). Behold, this is now the third day that the ship-master has occupied himself with fasting and prayer." The scribe quieted down and, on the fourth day, about the sixth hour, the ship-master got up and cried in a loud voice: "Glory to thee, Christ our God!"—and that in such a way that we were all astonished at his cry. And he said to the sailors: "Stretch out the skins," and whilst they were unfolding them, look! a cloud came over the ship and it rained enough water to satisfy all our needs. It was a great and fearful wonder, for as the ship was borne along by the wind, the cloud followed us; but it did not rain beyond the ship.

John Moschos, seventh century, Egypt/Palestine

Be present at our table, Lord;
Be here and everywhere adored;
Thy creatures bless, and grant that we
May feast in paradise with Thee.

John Cennick, 1718-1755, England

In [a second sense] this bread is the Word of God: "Not in bread alone doth man live, but in every word that proceedeth from the mouth of God." We pray, therefore, that He give us bread, that is, His Word. For this people derive that happiness which is a hunger for justice. For after spiritual things are considered, they are all the more desired; and this desire arouses a hunger, and from this hunger follows the fullness of life everlasting.

Thomas Aquinas, 1227?-1274?, Italy

Gracious Voices

Make us worthy, Lord,
    to serve those throughout the world who live and die in poverty
    or hunger.
Give then, through our hands, this day their daily bread;
    and by our understanding love, give peace and joy. Amen.

Mother Teresa of Calcutta, India

An old man and a brother led their life together. Now the old man was charitable. It happened that there was a famine and people came to his door seeking alms, and in charity the old man gave to all who came. Seeing what was happening, the brother said to the old man, "Give me my share of the loaves, and do what you like with yours." The old man divided the loaves and gave alms from his share. Now many people hastened to the old man, learning that he supplied everyone, and God—seeing that he supplied everyone—blessed these loaves. But when the brother had consumed his own food he said to the old man, "Since I have only a little food left, abba, take me back into the common life again." The old man said, "I will do as you wish." So they began again to live in common. When scarcity came again, the needy came back seeking alms. Now one day the brother came in and saw they were short of loaves. A poor man came, and the old man told the brother to give him alms. He said, "It is no longer possible, father." The old man said to him, "Go in and look." The brother went inside and found the bin full of loaves. When he saw that, he was filled with fear, and taking some he gave to the poor. In this way he learned the faith and virtue of the old man, and he gave glory to God.

a saying of the Desert Fathers, fourth-fifth centuries, Syria/Palestine/Egypt

Is not this the fast that I choose:
    to loose the bonds of injustice,
    to undo the thongs of the yoke,
to let the oppressed go free,
    and to break every yoke?
Is it not to share your bread with the hungry,
    and bring the homeless poor into your house;
when you see the naked, to cover them,
    and not to hide yourself from your own kin?

Isaiah 58:6-7

What, after all, are our most basic needs? For what do we yearn? This must not be psychologized or spiritualized in such a way as to evade the physical, emotional, and material needs of our life. We need nourishing food, warmth and shelter, healthy bodies and sane minds. We need strength and courage, and rest from our work; we need to be touched and held, to have companions with whom we can share joy and sorrow. We also yearn for justice and liberty, for dignity and respect. For all of these things we may pray. They are to us "daily bread."

But we do not need a fancier church building, a larger church membership, a new fur coat, victory for our football team, or the fear or adulation of our peers. A great deal of what passes for prayer is frivolous, springing from our utter confusion about what we need.

Theodore Jennings, United States

Gain all you can... Save all you can... Give all you can.

John Wesley, 1703-1791, England

99

CALLING TO
BAPTISM:

Professing
and Praying
with the
Church

FORGIVE US OUR SINS
AS WE FORGIVE THOSE WHO SIN AGAINST US.

Almighty and most merciful God,
we have erred and strayed from thy ways like lost sheep.
We have followed too much
the devices and desires of our own hearts.
We have offended against thy holy laws.
We have left undone
those things which we ought to have done,
and we have done
those things which we ought not to have done.
But thou, O Lord, have mercy upon us.
Spare thou those, O God, who confess their faults.
Restore thou those who are penitent,
according to thy promises declared in Christ Jesus our Lord.
And grant, O most merciful God, for his sake,
that we may hereafter live a godly, righteous, and sober life;
to the glory of thy holy name. Amen.

Prayer of Confession, United Methodist Hymnal

Augustine said:
   "Every individual will receive from God the amount of
   indulgence he has himself given to his neighbor."
Jerome said:
   "As God in Christ has forgiven us our sins, so let us also
   forgive those who sin against us."
Gregory said:
   "Only the one who has forgiven can seek forgiveness."
Isidore said:
   "In vain do they who neglect being reconciled with
   heir neighbors seek to be reconciled with God."
Caesarius said:
   "There is no trace of sin remaining in the soul that
   generously forgives the one who sins against it."

Defensor Grammaticus, seventh century, France

FORGIVE US THE WRONG WE HAVE DONE,
AS WE HAVE FORGIVEN THOSE WHO HAVE WRONGED US.
   When forgiveness is locked behind bared teeth
   When resentment hides behind an affable mask
   To forgive and to love are but inflated currency
   on the stock exchange of good manners.
   Wilt thou come to avenge or to forgive?
   Wilt thou come to strike down in vengeance
   or to lift up with a kiss?

Fridoline Ukur, Indonesia

Gracious Voices

Don't ever hurt one of your neighbors by using words in two senses. He could reply in the same way and you would both be wandering off the path of love.

Go to him and warn him with affectionate sincerity. When you have between you removed the cause of your unhappiness, you will both of you be free from anxiety and bitterness.

Don't recall to your memory anything your neighbor may have said in a moment of acrimony, whether he insulted you to your face, or spoke evil of you to another and that person has come and reported it to you. If you let yourself become angry, it is but a short step from anger to hatred.

Christ wants you never, in any way, for any reason, to cultivate a spirit of hatred, bitterness, anger or ill-feeling. The four gospels proclaim that on every page.

Only God is good by nature. The imitator of God is only good by intention, insofar as he wants to reconcile sinners with him who is good by nature. Therefore when they offend the imitator of God, he blesses them, and when they slander him, he prays for them. In short, he does everything possible not to stray far from the path of real love.

Maximus the Confessor, 580?-662, Asia Minor

Do not cause quarrels, but bring together and reconcile those who quarrel. Confess your sins. Do not go to prayer with an evil conscience.

Letter of Barnabas, second century

If we are not diseased, we do not want a cure. If we are not sick, why should we seek for a medicine to heal our sickness? What room is there to talk of our being renewed in "knowledge" or "holiness, after the image wherein we were created," if we never have lost that image? if we are as knowing and holy now, nay, far more so, than Adam was immediately after his creation? If, therefore, we take away this foundation, that man is by nature foolish and sinful, "fallen short of the glorious image of God," the Christian system falls at once; nor will it deserve so honorable an appellation, as that of a "cunningly devised fable."

John Wesley, 1703-1791, England

The work of purging the soul neither can nor should end except with our life itself. We must not be disturbed at our imperfections, since for us perfection consists in fighting against them. How can we fight against them unless we see them, or overcome them unless we face them?

Francis de Sales, 1567-1622, Switzerland

Only one petition in the Lord's Prayer has any condition attached to it: it is the petition for forgiveness.

William Temple, 1881-1944, England

CALLING TO
BAPTISM:

Professing
and Praying
with the
Church

The mercy of God is beyond description. While he is offering us a model prayer he is teaching us a way of life whereby we can be pleasing in his sight.

But that is not all. In this same prayer he gives us an easy method for attracting an indulgent and merciful judgment on our lives. He gives us the possibility of ourselves mitigating the sentence hanging over us and of compelling him to pardon us. What else could he do in the face of our generosity when we ask him to forgive as we have forgiven our neighbor?

If we are faithful in this prayer, each of us will ask forgiveness for our own failings after we have forgiven the sins of those who have sinned against us. I mean those who have sinned against us, not only those who have sinned against our Master.

There is, in fact, in some of us a very bad habit. We treat our sins against God, however appalling, with gentle indulgence: but when by contrast it is a matter of sins against us ourselves, albeit very tiny ones, we exact reparation with ruthless severity.

Anyone who has not forgiven from the bottom of the heart the brother or sister who has done him wrong will obtain from this prayer his own condemnation, rather than any mercy. It will be his own action that draws much more severe judgment on himself, seeing that in effect by these words we are asking God to behave as we have behaved ourselves.

Cassian, 360?-435?, Gaul

The more we learn to allow others to speak the Word to us, to accept humbly and gratefully even severe reproaches and admonitions, the more free and objective will we be in speaking ourselves. The person whose touchiness and vanity make him spurn a [brother's or sister's] earnest censure cannot speak the truth in humility to others; he is afraid of being rebuffed and of feeling that he has been aggrieved. The touchy person will always become a flatterer and very soon he will come to despise and slander his brother. But the humble person will stick both to truth and to love. He will stick to the Word of God and let it lead him to his [brother or sister]. Because he seeks nothing for himself and has no fears for himself, he can help his brother through the Word.

Reproof is unavoidable. God's Word demands it when a [brother or sister] falls into open sin. The practice of discipline in the congregation begins in the smallest circles. Where defection from God's Word in doctrine or life imperils the family fellowship and with it the whole congregation, the word of admonition and rebuke must be ventured. Nothing can be more cruel than the tenderness that consigns another to his sin. Nothing can be more compassionate than the severe rebuke that calls a [brother or sister] back from the path of sin. It is a ministry of mercy, an ultimate offer of genuine fellowship, when we allow nothing but God's Word to stand between us, judging and [consoling].

Dietrich Bonhoeffer, 1906-1945, Germany

Gracious Voices

102

And if any of you should at any time fall from what you now are, if you should again feel pride or unbelief, or any temper from which you are now delivered; do not deny, do not hide, do not disguise it at all, at the peril of your soul. At all events go to one in whom you can confide, and speak just what you feel. God will enable him to speak a word in season, which shall be health to your soul. And surely he will again lift up your head, and cause the bones that have been broken to rejoice.

John Wesley, 1703-1791, England

Peter came and said to him, "Lord, if another member of the church sins against me, how often should I forgive? As many as seven times?" Jesus said to him, "Not seven times, but, I tell you, seventy-seven times."

Matthew 18:21-22

And on the Lord's Day, after you have come together, break bread and offer the Eucharist, having first confessed your offences, so that your sacrifice may be pure. But let no one who has a quarrel with his neighbor join you until he is reconciled, lest your sacrifice be defiled. For it was said by the Lord: 'In every place and time let there be offered to me a clean sacrifice, because I am the great king': and also: 'and my name is wonderful among the Gentiles' (Malachi 1:11, 14).

Didache, second century

SAVE US FROM THE TIME OF TRIAL
AND DELIVER US FROM EVIL.

Lonely the boat, sailing at sea, tossed on a cold, stormy night;
cruel the sea which seemed so wide, with waves so high.
This single ship sailed the deep sea, straight into the gale;
O Lord, great is the peril, dangers do all assail.

"Storms in our lives, cruel and cold, surely will arise again,
threatening lives, threatening us on life's wild sea.
Powerful and great, God's hand is there, firmly in control.
O Lord, calm peace comes from you, peace comes to my lone soul."

Helen Kim, 1899-1970, Korea

The treasures of this world may well be compared to husks, for they have no kernal in them, and they that feed upon them may soon stuff their throats, but cannot fill their bellies. They may be choked by them, but cannot be satisfied with them.

Anne Bradstreet, 1612-1672, New England

An old man was asked, "What is humility?" He replied, "It is when your brother sins against you and you forgive him before he comes to ask for forgiveness."

a saying of the Desert Fathers, fourth-fifth centuries, Syria/Palestine/Egypt

CALLING TO
BAPTISM:

Professing
and Praying
with the
Church

If a man is doing something according to God, trial of some kind will come upon him, for trial and temptation either precede or follow all good. Neither is it sure the thing is happening according to God, unless it is proved so by trials and temptations. . . . As shadows accompany the bodies that cast them, so temptations accompany the fulfillment of the commandments.

Dorotheus of Gaza, sixth century

The request "Lead us not into temptation" raises a difficult problem. If we pray God not to allow us to be tempted, what opportunity shall we have to give him proof of our steadfastness and fidelity? For it is written: "Blessed is the one who endures temptation and overcomes it." (see James 1:12)

Then what is the meaning of this phrase? It does not mean: do not allow us to come into temptation. It means: when we come into temptation, let us not be defeated by it.

Job was tempted but he did not give way to the temptation. In fact, he did not accuse the divine Wisdom, he did not go down the road of blasphemy to which the Tempter wanted to attract him.

Abraham was tempted, and Joseph was tempted. But neither one nor the other yielded to the temptation, because neither of them said "yes" to the Tempter.

So praying the Lord's Prayer is like saying: "Together with the temptation, give us also the strength to overcome it." (I Corinthians 10:13)

Cassian, 360?-435?, Gaul

So great are the trials, and so profound the darkness, spiritual as well as corporal, through which souls must pass, if they will attain to perfection, that no human learning can explain them, nor experience describe them. He only who has passed through them can know them, but even he cannot explain them.

John of the Cross, 1542-1591, Spain

But it may be observed, that the Son of God does not destroy the whole work of the devil in man, as long as he remains in this life. He does not yet destroy bodily weakness, sickness, pain, and a thousand infirmities incident to flesh and blood. He does not destroy all that weakness of understanding, which is the natural consequence of the soul's dwelling in a corruptible body. . . . It is to remove from us all temptation to pride, and all thought of independency, (which is the very thing that men in general so earnestly covet under the name of liberty), that he leaves us encompassed with all these infirmities, particularly weakness of understanding; till the sentence takes place, "Dust thou art, and unto dust thou shalt return!"

John Wesley, 1703-1791, England

Gracious Voices

The Lord's Prayer has an ending which neatly summarizes the different requests. We say actually at the end: "But deliver us from evil," understanding by such an expression everything that the Enemy can devise against us in this world.

One certain conviction we have: that God is a powerful support since he grants his help to anyone who asks for it.

Consequently, when we say: "Deliver us from evil," there is nothing else left for us to ask. Invoking the protection of God against evil means asking for everything we need.

This prayer secures us against any kind of machination of the devil and of the world. Who could be afraid of the world if he has God as his protector?

You see, brothers and sisters, how amazing the Lord's Prayer is. It is truly a compendium of all the requests we could possibly make.

Our Lord Jesus Christ who came for all people, for the wise as for the ignorant, without distinction of sex or age, reduces the precepts of salvation to the essential minimum. He wants even the simplest to be able to understand and remember them.

Cyprian of Carthage, 200?-258, North Africa

Deliver us from the Evil One. That is the ultimate petition. Never mind the temptations. We know they're out there and we know we'll strike at the baited lure of Satan and Caesar, become ensnarled in the pseudo-sophistication and false security of their offerings. Caesar and the Devil are powerful. But only second best.

Will Campbell, United States

Hear a just cause, O LORD; attend to my cry;
  give ear to my prayer from lips free of deceit.
From you let my vindication come;
  let your eyes see the right. . . .
I call upon you, for you will answer me, O God;
  incline your ear to me, hear my words.
Wondrously show your steadfast love,
  O savior of those who seek refuge
  from their adversaries at your right hand.
Guard me as the apple of the eye;
  hide me in the shadow of your wings.

Psalm 17:1-2, 6-8

You should not wait until you are cleansed of wandering thoughts before you desire to pray: such distraction is not banished from the mind except by assiduous prayer entailing much labor. If you only begin on prayer when you see that your mind has become perfect and exalted above all recollection of the world, then you will never pray.

Isaac of Nineveh, seventh century, East Syria

An old man said, "What condemns us is not that thoughts enter into us but that we use them badly; indeed, through our thoughts we can be ship-wrecked, and through our thoughts we can be crowned."

a saying of the Desert Fathers

CALLING TO
BAPTISM:

Professing
and Praying
with the
Church

One of the saints said:

When we pray to the Lord and say *Lead us not into temptation*, we are not saying this so that we shall not be tried; that would be impossible. We are praying not to be overcome by temptation to the extent of doing something displeasing to God. That is what it means not to enter temptation. The holy martyrs were tried by their torments but, as they were not overcome by them, they did not enter into temptation, any more than someone who fights with a beast and is not devoured by it. When he is devoured, then he has entered into temptation. So it is with every passion, so long as one is not overcome by that passion.

John Moschos, seventh century, Egypt/Palestine

He taught us to ask the Father to deliver us from the Evil One. And shortly thereafter he became the instrument of the deliverance through his execution and resurrection. The last enemy was conquered—death. The power of Satan is broken. We are delivered from the Evil One. Hallelujah!

Will Campbell, United States

The human heart is like a ship on a stormy sea driven about by winds blowing from all four corners of heaven. In one person, there is fear and anxiety about impending disaster; another groans and moans at all the surrounding evil. One mingles hope and presumption out of the good fortune to which he is looking forward; and another is puffed up with such a confidence and pleasure in his present possessions. Such storms, however, teach us to speak sincerely and frankly, and make a clean breast. For one who is in the grip of fear or distress speaks of disaster in quite a different way from one who is filled with happiness; and one who is filled with joy speaks and sings about happiness quite differently from one who is in the grip of fear. . . .

The Book of Psalms is full of heartfelt utterances made during storms of this kind. Where can one find nobler words to express joy than in the Psalms of praise or gratitude? In them you can see into the hearts of all the saints as if you were looking at a lovely pleasure-garden, or were gazing into heaven. How fair and charming and delightful are the flowers you will find there which grow out of all kinds of beautiful thoughts of God and his grace. Or where can one find more profound, more penitent, more sorrowful words in which to express grief than in the Psalms of lamentation? In these you see into the hearts of all the saints as if you were looking at death or gazing into hell, so dark and obscure is the scene rendered by the changing shadows of the wrath of God.

Martin Luther, 1483-1546, Germany

Gracious Voices

Two old men had lived together for many years and had never fought with one another. The first said to the other, "Let us also have a fight like other men do." The other replied, "I do not know how to fight." The first said to him, "Look, I will put a brick between us, and I will say it is mine, and you say, 'No, it is mine,' and so the fight will begin." So they put a brick between them and the first said, "This brick is mine," and the other said, "No, it is mine," and the first responded, "If it is yours, take it and go"—so they gave it up without being able to find an occasion for argument.

a saying of the Desert Fathers, fourth-fifth centuries, Syria/Palestine/Egypt

An old man said, "I would rather have a defeat with humility than a victory with pride."

a saying of the Desert Fathers, fourth-fifth centuries, Syria/ Palestine/Egypt

O thou, from whom to be turned is to fall,
    to whom to be turned is to rise,
    and in whom to stand is to abide for ever;
Grant us in all our duties thy help,
    in all our perplexities thy guidance,
    in all our dangers thy protection,
    and in all our sorrows thy peace;
    through Jesus Christ our Lord.

Augustine, 354-430, North Africa

Precious Lord, take my hand,
lead me on, let me stand,
I am tired, I am weak, I am worn;
through the storm, through the night, lead me on to the light;
Take my hand, precious Lord, lead me home.

Thomas A. Dorsey, 1899-1965, United States

Almighty and everlasting God,
    who can banish all affliction both of soul and of body,
show forth your power upon those in need,
that by your mercy they may be restored to serve you afresh
    in holiness of living, through Jesus Christ our Lord. Amen.

May the power of God's indwelling presence heal you
of all illnesses—
    of body, mind, spirit, and relationships—
that you may serve God with a loving heart. Amen.

prayers from A Service of Healing

CALLING TO
BAPTISM:

*Professing
and Praying
with the
Church*

FOR THE KINGDOM, THE POWER,
AND THE GLORY ARE YOURS
NOW AND FOR EVER. AMEN.

We are dependent on God's power through every step of our redemption. We are dependent on the power of God to convert us, and give faith in Jesus Christ, and the new nature.

Jonathan Edwards, 1703-1758, New England

"I am the Alpha and the Omega," says the Lord God,
who is, and who was, and who is to come, the Almighty.

"Worthy is the Lamb that was slaughtered
to receive power and wealth and wisdom and might
and honor and glory and blessing!"

Revelation 1:8, 5:12

Immortal, invisible, God only wise,
in light inaccessible hid from our eyes,
most blessed, most glorious, the Ancient of Days,
almighty, victorious, thy great name we praise.

Thou reignest in glory; thou dwellest in light;
thine angels adore thee, all veiling their sight;
all laud we would render: O help us to see
'tis only the splendor of light hideth thee.

Walter C. Smith, 1824-1908, Scotland

Clap your hands, all you peoples;
  shout to God with loud songs of joy.
For the LORD, the Most High, is awesome,
  a great king over all the earth.

Psalm 47:1-2

Yea, Amen! Let all adore thee, high on thy eternal throne;
Savior, take the power and glory,
claim the kingdom for thine own.
Hallelujah! Hallelujah! Hallelujah! Everlasting God, come down!

Charles Wesley, 1707-1788, England

Gracious Voices

It happened that a fire broke out backstage in a theater. The clown came out to inform the public. They thought it was just a jest and applauded. He repeated his warning, they shouted even louder. So I think the world will come to an end amid general applause from all the wits, who believe that it is a joke.

Søren Kierkegaard, 1813-1855, Denmark

O Consuming Fire, Spirit of Love, "come upon me," and create in my soul a kind of incarnation of the Word: that I may be another humanity for Him in which He can renew His whole Mystery. And You, O Father, bend lovingly over Your poor little creature, "cover her with Your shadow," seeing in her only the "Beloved in whom You are well pleased."

O my Three, my All, my Beatitude, infinite Solitude, Immensity in which I lose myself, I surrender to You as Your prey. Bury Yourself in me that I may bury myself in You until I depart to contemplate in Your light the abyss of Your greatness.

Elizabeth of the Trinity, 1880-1906, France

Just as Moses once spoke to God as friend to friend, and God answered him (Exodus 33:11), so now the Word and the soul converse with mutual enjoyment, like two friends. And no wonder. The two streams of their love have but one single source from which they are sustained. Winged words, honey-sweet, fly to and fro between them, and their eyes, like heralds of holy love, betray to each other their fullness of delight. He calls her his dearest one, proclaims her beauty, and repeats that proclamation—only to win a like response from her.

Bernard of Clairvaux, 1090-1153, France

To God be the glory, great things he hath done!
So loved he the world that he gave us his Son,
who yielded his life an atonement for sin, and
opened the lifegate that all may go in.
Praise the Lord, praise the Lord, let the earth hear his voice!
Praise the Lord, praise the Lord, let the people rejoice!
O come to the Father through Jesus the Son,
and give him the glory, great things he hath done!

Fanny J. Crosby, 1820-1915, United States

The first ideas I can remember date back to when I was five years old. When I went to bed, instead of sleeping—I have never been much of a sleeper—I used to think about eternity. I would think "forever, forever, forever." I would try to imagine enormous distances and pile still more distances on these and realize they would never come to an end.

Anthony Mary Claret, 1807-1870, Spain

How swiftly passes away the glory of the world.

Thomas a Kempis, 1380?-1471, Germany

CALLING TO
BAPTISM:

Professing
and Praying
with the
Church

O burning Mountain, O chosen Sun,
O perfect Moon, O fathomless Well,
O unattainable Height, O Clearness beyond measure;
O Wisdom without end, O Mercy without limit,
O Strength beyond resistance, O Crown beyond all majesty:
The humblest thing you created sings your praise.

Mecthild of Magdeburg, 1212-1283, Germany

Almighty God, I long for a just sense of Thee as Father, Son and Holy Spirit. After so many years of inquiry, so long reading and so much thinking, Thy boundless essence appears more inexplicable, the perfection of Thy glory more bright and inaccessible. Thy sublimity transcends all thought; words cannot express what is so far above their nature; therefore the simplest and plainest are the best.

I cannot do Thee the justice that I would. I cannot, by the utmost force and energy of all my powers, attain to the proper knowledge of Thine essence, Thine essential glory, wherein all perfections concenter. Yet enable me to discover the emanations of that glory; the manifestations it hath made or maketh of itself, in the exercise of Thy Divine perfections, in the creation of the world, the redemption and regeneration of our human nature and the government of the world, particularly in respect to humankind. Amen.

Susanna Wesley, 1669-1742, England

Hath any man hope that he is converted, and sanctified, and that his mind is endowed with true excellency and spiritual beauty, and his sins forgiven, and he received into God's favor, and exalted to the honor and blessedness of being his child, and an heir of eternal life; let him give God all the glory.

Jonathan Edwards, 1703-1758, New England

A life of faith is a life of gratitude—it means a life in which I am willing to experience my complete dependence upon God and to praise and thank him unceasingly for the gift of being. A truly eucharistic life means saying thanks to God, always praising God, and always being more surprised by the abundance of God's goodness and love. How can such a life not also be a joyful life? It is the truly converted life in which God has become the center of all. There gratitude is joy and joy is gratitude and everything becomes a surprising sign of God's presence.

Henri J. M. Nouwen, 1932-1996, United States

Gracious Voices

THE BAPTISMAL BATH: WATER OF DEATH AND LIFE

Pour out your Holy Spirit to bless this gift of water and those who receive it.

You are standing in front of God and in the presence of the host of angels. The Holy Spirit is about to impress his seal on each of your souls. You are about to be pressed into the service of the great king.

Cyril of Jerusalem, 313?-386

Baptism is the initiatory sacrament, which enters us into covenant with God. It was instituted by Christ, who alone has power to institute a proper sacrament, a sign, seal, pledge, and means of grace, perpetually obligatory on all Christians.

John Wesley, 1703-1791, England

Wash, O God, our sons and daughters,
  where your cleansing waters flow.
Number them among your people;
  bless as Christ blessed long ago.
Weave them garments bright and sparkling;
  compass them with love and light.
Fill, anoint them; send your Spirit,
  holy dove and heart's delight.

Ruth Duck, United States

As many of you as were baptized into Christ have clothed yourselves with Christ. There is no longer Jew or Greek, there is no longer slave or free, there is no longer male and female; for all of you are one in Christ Jesus. And if you belong to Christ, then you are Abraham's offspring, heirs according to the promise.

Galatians 3:27-29

Pour out your Holy Spirit,
to bless this gift of water and *those* who *receive* it,
to wash away *their* sin
  and clothe *them* in righteousness
  throughout *their* lives,
that, dying and being raised with Christ,
  they may share in his final victory.

Thanksgiving over the Water, Baptismal Covenant

111

Therefore, O blessed ones, you for whom the grace of God is waiting, when you come up from that most sacred washing of the new birth (Titus 3:5) and for the first time spread out your hands with your brethren in your mother's house, ask your Father, ask the Lord, as a special gift, for an abundance of spiritual gifts (I Corinthians 12:1-31). "Ask" he says, "and you will receive." Now that you have searched and found, knocked and it has been opened for you, I ask only that, as you ask, that you will remember Tertullian, a sinner.

Tertullian, 160?-230?, North Africa

My teenage daughter, who for days on end appears to care not a tittle about what clothing covers her body, recently went to the prom. Preparations began six weeks in advance; she had her dress, in fact, before she had a date. The desired dark green lace mini-dress was, amazingly, found, and on sale. The green dangle earrings at the vintage clothing store could, indeed, be converted to studs for her pierced ears. The 1930's-style high heeled suede pumps were a find. And lest I think that only females care about clothing, her date arrived in his rented tuxedo replete with a Mickey Mouse vest and bow tie. Until midnight, tattered jeans and washed-out T-shirts were transmogrified by a fairy godmother's wand . . .

If in the liturgy we wear Christ and Christ wears us, how will it be? What would that be like, we gladly clothed in Christ, and Christ proudly showing us off to God? Perhaps the liturgy is most like my daughter's prom. For those hours we are transformed. Everyone is wearing a colorful bow to celebrate the event. A Spirit in us makes us move beautifully. We are part of a whole. We are joyful, the dance is glorious, and all of us being here is a delight.

Gail Ramshaw, United States

The strange, the extraordinary, thing [in baptism] is that we did not really die, nor were really buried or really crucified; nor did we really rise again: this was figurative and symbolic; yet our salvation was real. Christ's crucifixion was real, His burial was real, and His resurrection was real; and all these He has freely made ours, that by sharing His sufferings in a symbolic enactment we may really and truly gain salvation. Oh, too generous love! Christ received the nails in His immaculate hands and feet; Christ felt the pain: and on me without pain or labor, through the fellowship of His pain, He freely bestows salvation.

Cyril of Jerusalem, 313?-386

Gracious Voices

There is one body and one Spirit, just as you were called to the one hope of your calling, one Lord, one faith, one baptism, one God and Father of all, who is above all and through all and in all.

Ephesians 4:4-6

Therefore, baptism is a struggle to conquer sin throughout one's whole life. Whoever now finds behind him the Pharoah (that is, persecution, tribulation, fear and need) and in front of him the sea (that is, the helplessness of all creatures) and concludes that he has been abandoned by God and sees nothing other than death, stands in the true baptism to which he consented before God and his community or people by the symbol of baptism.

Hans Hut, ?–1527, Germany

In the midst of our everyday continuing *sins,* we should remember that baptism has washed our *Sin* and take comfort. This is repentance. Not that we do not continue to be and do wrong. We still sin. But, as Paul said, we no longer live by Sin, hide from it, attempt to explain it away. We can afford to be so pessimistic about human nature because we are so optimistic about God's grace in restoring our rightful vocation. Sin no longer determines us. We come out of the waters as new creatures. Our cleansed lives are given back to us, fresh and new, ready to be begun again. We are no longer anxious and afraid. We can breathe. *We are free.*

William Willimon, United States

But when the goodness and loving kindness of God our Savior appeared, he saved us, not because of any works of righteousness that we had done, but according to his mercy, through the water of rebirth and renewal by the Holy Spirit. This Spirit he poured out on us richly through Jesus Christ our Savior, so that, having been justified by his grace, we might become heirs according to the hope of eternal life. The saying is sure.

Titus 3:4–8

"I have come to give myself up," he said.
"It is well," said Mother Kirk. "You have come a long way round to reach this place, whither I would have carried you in a few moments. But it is very well."
"What must I do?" said John.
"You must take off your rags," said she, "as your friend has done already, and then you must dive into this water."
"Alas," said he, "I have never learned to dive."
"There is nothing to learn," said she. "The art of diving is not to do anything new but simply to cease doing something. You have only to let yourself go."

C. S. Lewis, 1898–1963, England

I am the vine, you are the branches. Those who abide in me and I in them bear much fruit, because apart from me, you can do nothing.

John 15:5

INITIATION:
Joined to Christ and the Church

The persons who become members of the Methodist societies in America are first introduced to the class, which they attend for six months on probation; at the extirpation of which, if their conduct has been consistent with their professions, they are baptised, and accounted full members of the society. After I had completed my six months probation, I was baptised by the Rev. Joseph Lybrand; and I shall never forget the heavenly impression I felt on that joyfully solemn occasion. Truly the one Spirit of Jesus doth by means of His ministers, baptise us into the one body of Jesus. I Corinthians 12:13. When he said, "I baptise thee into the name of the Father, Son, and Holy Ghost, Amen," I was so overwhelmed with the love of God, that self seemed annihilated: I was completely lost and absorbed in the divine fascinations. The Rev. Divine then added, "Be thou faithful unto death, and thou shalt receive a crown of life; and 'Whatsoever thy hand findeth to do, do with all might' (Ecclesiastes 9:10); for this is the will of God in Christ Jesus concerning you." I was now accounted a full member of the society, and privileged with the communion of the Lord's Supper.

Zilpha Elaw, 1790?-?, United States

Do you not know that all of us who have been baptized into Christ Jesus were baptized into his death? Therefore we have been buried with him by baptism into death, so that, just as Christ was raised from the dead by the glory of the Father, so we too might walk in newness of life.

Romans 6:3-4

Among the local taverns there'll be a slack in bus'ness,
'cause Jesse's drinkin' came before the groc'ries and the rent.
Among the local women there'll be a slack in cheatin',
Cause Jesse won't be steppin' out again.

The scars on Jesse's knuckles were more than just respected,
the county courthouse records tell all there is to tell.
The pockets of the gamblers will soon miss Jesse's money,
And the black eye of the law will soon be well.

From now on Nancy Taylor can proudly speak to neighbors,
and tell them how much Jesse took up with little Jim.
Now Jimmy's got a daddy and Jesse's got a fam'ly,
And Franklin County's got a lot more man.

Gracious Voices

They baptized Jesse Taylor in Cedar Creek last Sunday;
Jesus gained a soul and Satan lost a good right arm.
They all cried hallelujah when Jesse's head went under,
'cause this time he went under for the Lord.

Dallas Frazier, United States

So when I am baptized and put my head under the water, I wish to receive the death and burial of Christ our Lord, and I solemnly profess my faith in his resurrection; when I come up out of the water, this is a sign that I believe I am already risen.

Theodore of Mopsuestia, 350?-428, West Syria

Thus the person is made quite clean and innocent, sacramentally, which means that he has received the sign of God, namely baptism. This indicates that all his sins are dead, and that he will die in grace and rise again on the Last Day, pure and free from sin, to live eternally. Thus it is true that, because of the sacrament, he is pure and free from sin, but as this is not yet perfected and he is still living in sinful flesh, he is not yet free from sin or pure from all things, but has begun to be made pure and innocent.

But you may say: but what help is baptism to me if it does not completely slay my sin and wash me clean? Here follows the right to understanding and knowledge of the sacrament of baptism.

First, that you submit to the sacrament and its meaning shows that you desire to die to sin and be made new on the last Day in accordance with the meaning of the sacrament. God accepts this and permits you to be baptized, and from that hour He begins to make you new. He pours into you His grace and the Holy Spirit, who begins to kill your sinful nature and to prepare you to die and rise again on the Last Day.

Further, if you promise to remain thus, and more and more to overcome sin, so long as you live, even until death, God accepts that and prepares you through all your earthly life with many good works and with much suffering. Thus He does what you desired in baptism, and your desire was to be redeemed from sin, and to die and rise on the Last Day in newness of life, and thus to complete the meaning of your baptism.

Martin Luther, 1483-1546, Germany

Now is the moment I am beginning to be a disciple. May nothing seen or unseen begrudge me making my way to Jesus Christ. Come fire, cross, battling with wild beasts, wrenching of my bones, mangling of limbs, crushing of my whole body, cruel tortures of the devil—only let me get to Jesus Christ! Not the wide bounds of earth nor the kingdoms of this world will avail me anything. I would rather die and get to Jesus Christ, than reign over the ends of the earth. That is whom I am looking for—the one who died for us. That is whom I want—the one who rose for us. I am going through the pangs of being born.

Ignatius of Antioch, first century

So also you must consider yourselves dead to sin and alive to God in Christ Jesus.

Romans 6:11

Christ is being baptized. The one who is Christ is there, and the one who is John, and the dim other people standing on cobbles or sitting on beach logs back from the bay. These are ordinary people—if I am one now, if those are ordinary sheep singing a song in the pasture.

The two men are bare to the waist. The one walks him into the water, and holds him under. His hand is on his neck. Christ is coiled and white under the water, standing on stones.

He lifts from the water. Water beads on his shoulders. I see water in balls as heavy as planets, a billion beads of water as weighty as worlds, and he lifts them up on his back as he rises. He stands wet in the water. Each one bead is transparent, and each has a world, or the same world, light and alive and apparent inside the drop: it is all there ever could be, moving at once, past and future, and all the people. I can look into any sphere and see people stream past me, and cool my eyes with colors and the sight of the world in spectacle perishing ever, and ever renewed. I do; I deepen into a drop and see all that time contains, all the faces and deeps of the worlds and all the earth's contents, every landscape and room, everything living or made or fashioned, all past and future stars, and especially faces, faces like the cells of everything, faces pouring past me talking, and going, and gone. And I am gone.

For outside it is bright. The surface of things outside the drops has fused. Christ himself and the others, and the brown warm wind, and hair, sky, the beach, the shattered water—all this has fused. It is the one glare of holiness; it is bare and unspeakable. There is no speech nor language; there is nothing, no one thing, nor motion, nor time. There is only this everything. There is only this, and its bright and multiple noise.

Annie Dillard, United States

But you are a chosen race, a royal priesthood, a holy nation, God's own people, in order that you may proclaim the mighty acts of him who called you out of darkness into his marvelous light.
    Once you were not a people,
        but now you are God's people;
    once you had not received mercy,
        but now you have received mercy.

1 Peter 2:9-10

Gracious Voices

Ritual action has the power to communicate and incorporate. That is how God has made us; and that is why God has given us sacraments—divine gifts designed to match a capacity put within us at creation. Baptism is not merely an audiovisual aid, soon forgotten. It is a sign that brings to pass, by the power of the Holy Spirit, the very identity it proclaims.

Laurence Hull Stookey, United States

The sign is far more than a subjective experience. It is an objective act bound up with the faithful promise of God. That Christians experience deep personal feelings related to faith, there can be no doubt, but faith cannot rest on feelings. Otherwise, when we are in a happy mood we consider that God is good, loving, and gracious, but when depression overtakes us we begin to suspect God is cold, distant, and stingy. The identity the Holy Spirit gives us is far more stable than that. To be baptized is to be incorporated into the God who is gracious whether we happen to feel like it on a certain day or not. When feelings fail, we can rely upon the sign and thus find strength.

Laurence Hull Stookey, United State

Do not fear, for I have redeemed you; I have called you by name, you are mine.

Isaiah 43:1

When we are baptized, we (like the first disciples) jump on a moving train. As disciples, we do not so much accept a creed, or come to a clear sense of self-understanding by which we know this or that with utter certitude. We become part of a journey that began long before we got here and shall continue long after we are gone. Too often, we have conceived of salvation—what God does to us in Jesus—as a purely personal decision, or a matter of finally getting our heads straight on basic beliefs, or of having some inner feelings of righteousness about ourselves and God, or of having our social attitudes readjusted. . . . salvation is not so much a new beginning but rather a beginning in the middle, so to speak. Faith begins, not in discovery, but in remembrance. The story began without us, as a story of the peculiar way God is redeeming the world, a story that invites us to come forth and be saved by sharing in the work of a new people whom God has created in Israel and Jesus. Such movement saves us by (1) placing us within an adventure that is nothing less than God's purpose for the whole world, and (2) communally training us to fashion our lives in accordance with what is true rather than what is false.

Stanley Hauerwas and William Willimon, United States

Christians are the Holy Nation under the new covenant; they are men, women, and children to whom God has given a new "nationality" by taking them into the one new Man. The new covenant involves a new relationship with God, which is embodied in Jesus the Christ and which is shared with those who are taken up into the "body" of the Christ.

The action by which men accept this new covenant with God, and by which God puts them into it, is baptism. Baptism can only be understood in terms of faith: of trust in God and surrender to him by men, and of faithfulness on God's part because he abides by the Covenant established in Jesus the new creation and, accepting our submission, places us within that new covenant. . . .

The new covenant is therefore the baptismal covenant. It gives us a way of life and a way of work which is new because it is the way of the New Covenant, Jesus, through and upon men and women in the world of time and change.

Dom Robert Petitpierre, England

To *remember* our baptism is not primarily a matter of recalling a consciously experienced dramatic event. Such a consciously recalled "converting experience" may be a crucial part of the history of the baptized person's life, but it is only one moment in a whole process. Some Christian traditions have held that one must first consciously experience and witness to saving faith *before* the baptismal action of the church is administered. Others have emphasized that the baptismal action with water and in the name of God with the laying on of hands (and anointing) will elicit a specific faith response over time. The latter view assumes a faithful church whose members support, nourish, and sustain a lively sense of the dying and rising with Christ as the environment into which infants may grow until, as more mature persons, they come to profess their own faith and experience. In the case of persons whose baptism is preceded by strong converting experiences, the rites have a more direct expressive power and witness to the faith professed by the individual and the church together.

In all cases of genuine baptismal life in Christ, however, to remember our baptism is a matter of recognition of all that God has done and is yet to do in our lives.

Don Saliers, United States

What does being baptized into his death mean? It has to do with our dying as he did. We do this by our baptism, for baptism is the cross. What the cross is to Christ, baptism is to us. Christ died in the flesh; we have died to sin. Both are deaths, and both are real.

But if it is real, what is our part, what must we contribute? Paul goes on to say, "As Christ was raised up from the dead by the glory of the Father, even so we also should walk in newness of life" (Romans 6:4). Here Paul tells of the importance of the resurrection.

Do you believe that Christ was raised from the dead? Believe the same of yourself. Just as his death is yours, so also is his resurrection; if you have shared in the one, you shall share in the other. As of now the sin is done away with.

Paul sets before us a demand: to bring about a newness of life by a changing of habits. For when the fornicator becomes chaste, when the covetous person becomes merciful, when the harsh become subdued, a resurrection has taken place, a prelude to the final resurrection which is to come.

How is it a resurrection? It is a resurrection because sin has been mortified, and righteousness has risen in its place; the old life has passed away, and new, angelic life, is now being lived.

John Chrysostom, 345-407, West Syria

Gracious Voices

The preacher was standing about ten feet out in the stream where the water came up to his knees. He was a tall youth in khaki trousers that he had rolled up higher than the water. He had on a blue shirt and a red scarf around his neck but no hat and his light-colored hair was cut in sideburns that curved into the hollows of his cheeks. His face was all bone and red light reflected from the river. He looked as if he might have been nineteen years old. He was singing in a high twangy voice, above the singing on the bank, and he kept his hands behind him and his head tilted back.

He ended the hymn on a high note and stood silent, looking down at the water and shifting his feet in it. Then he looked up at the people on the bank. They stood close together, waiting; their faces were solemn but expectant and every eye was on him. He shifted his feet again.

"Maybe I know why you come," he said in the twangy voice, "maybe I don't."

"If you ain't come for Jesus, you ain't come for me. If you just come to see can you leave your pain in the river, you ain't come for Jesus. You can't leave your pain in the river," he said. "I never told nobody that." He stopped and looked down at his knees.

"I seen you cure a woman oncet!" a sudden high voice shouted from the hump of people. "Seen that woman git up and walk out straight where she had limped in!"

The preacher lifted one foot and then the other. He seemed almost but not quite to smile. "You might as well go home if that's what you come for," he said.

Then he lifted his head and arms and shouted, "Listen to what I got to say, you people! There ain't but one river and that's the River of Life, made out of Jesus' Blood. That's the river you have to lay your pain in, in the River of Faith, in the River of Life, in the River of Love, in the rich red river of Jesus' Blood, you people!"

His voice grew soft and musical. "All the rivers come from that one River and go back to it like it was the ocean sea and if you believe, you can lay your pain in that River and get rid of it because that's the River that was made to carry sin. It's a River full of pain itself, pain itself, moving toward the Kingdom of Christ, to be washed away, slow, you people, slow as this here old red water river round my feet.

"Listen," he sang, "I read in Mark about an unclean man, I read in Luke about a blind man, I read in John about a dead man! Oh you people hear! The same blood that makes this River red, made that leper clean, made that blind man stare, made that dead man leap! You people with trouble," he cried, "lay it in that River of Blood, lay it in that River of Pain, and watch it move away toward the Kingdom of Christ."

Flannery O'Connor, 1925-1964, United States

Batter my heart, three person'd God; for, you As yet but knocke, breathe, shine, and seeke to mend; That I may rise, and stand, o'erthrow mee,' and bend Your force, to breake, blowe, burn and make me new.

John Donne, 1573-1631, England

THE EUCHARISTIC MEAL: FEAST OF JOY

Pour out your Holy Spirit on us gathered here, and on these gifts of bread and wine. Make them be for us the body and blood of Christ.

As a woman, compelled by natural affection, hastens to feed her babe from her overflowing breast, so also Christ ever nourishes with His Blood those whom He regenerates.

John Chrysostom, 345?-407, West Syria

O Thou who this mysterious bread didst in Emmaus break, return, herewith our souls to feed, and to thy followers speak.

Charles Wesley, 1707-1788, England

Whenever you receive the body and blood of Jesus in the Eucharist, his love is given to you, the same love that he showed on the cross. It is the love of God for all people of all times and places, all religions and creeds, all races and classes, all tribes and nations, all sinners and saints.

Henri J. M. Nouwen, 1932-1996, United States

I believe, that Thou hast instituted and ordained holy mysteries, as pledges of thy love, and for a continual commemoration of Thy death; that Thou hast not only given Thyself to die for me, but to be my spiritual food and sustenance in that holy sacrament to my great and endless comfort. O may I frequently approach Thy altar with humility and devotion, and work in me all those holy and heavenly affections, which become the remembrance of a crucified Savior.

Richard Allen, 1760-1831, United States

Father of earth and heaven,
    Thy hungry children feed,
Thy grace be to our spirits given,
    That true, immortal bread.
Grant us and all our race
    In Jesus Christ to prove
The sweetness of thy pardoning grace,
    The manna of thy love.

Charles Wesley, 1707-1788, England

Gracious Voices

Now the silence
Now the peace
Now the empty hands uplifted
Now the kneeling
Now the plea
Now the Father's arms in welcome
Now the hearing
Now the power
Now the vessel brimmed for pouring
Now the body
Now the blood
Now the joyful celebration
Now the wedding
Now the songs
Now the heart forgiven leaping
Now the Spirit's visitation
Now the Son's epiphany
Now the Father's blessing
Now
Now
Now

Jaroslav J. Vajda, United States

In fact, contact with God is the true sacrament.

Simone Weil, 1909-1943, France

The Lord's Supper ought to be more firmly regarded from the Easter standpoint, than is generally the case. It is not primarily a mourning or funeral meal, but the anticipation of the marriage feast of the Lamb. The Supper is a joyous meal: the eating of His, Jesus Christ's, flesh and the drinking of His blood is meat and drink unto life eternal in the midst of our life. We are guests at His table and so no longer separated from Himself. Thus in this sign the witness of His meal is united to the witness of the Holy Spirit. It tells us really, you shall not die but live, and proclaim the Lord's works! *You!* We are guests at the Lord's Table, which is not only an image, it is an event. 'Whosoever believeth on me, hath the life eternal.' Your death is put to death. You are in fact already dead. The terror you face you have already completely behind you. You may live as a guest at this table. You may go in the strength of this food forty days and forty nights. In this strength it is possible. Let this prevail, that you have drunk and eaten; let all that is deadly around you be conquered. Do not nurse your sorrow tenderly; do not make a little garden of it with an overhanging weeping willow! 'We do but make the cross and pain the greater by our melancholy.' We are called to a quite different situation. 'If we died with Christ, we believe that we shall also live with Him' (Romans 6:8). The one who believes that is already beginning here and now to live the complete life.

Karl Barth, 1886-1968, Switzerland

With Thine Image stamped of old,
Find Thy coin more choice than gold;
Known to Thee by name, recall
To Thee Thy home-sick prodigal.

Sacrifice and Offering
None there is that I can bring;
None, save what is Thine alone:
I bring Thee, Lord, but of Thine Own—

Broken Body, Blood Outpoured,
These I bring, my God, my Lord;
Wine of Life, and Living Bread,
With these for me Thy Board is spread.

Christina Rossetti, 1830-1894, England

Sanctify me by your Mysteries,
illumine my mind with knowledge of you,
make your hope to shine out in my heart,
hold me worthy to supplicate for it,
O God my Father and Lord of my life;
illumine your lamp within me,
place in me what belongs to you
so that I may forget what belongs to myself.
Cast upon me the constraint
of wonder of you,
so that the constraint of nature
may be overpowered by it.
Stir up within me
the vision of your Mysteries
so that I may become aware of what was placed in me
at holy baptism.
You paved within me a Guide:
may he show me your glory
at all times.

Isaac of Nineveh, seventh century, East Syria

"For we, who are many, are one bread, one body" (1 Corinthians 10:17). "For why speak I of communion?" says he, "we are that self-same body." For what is the bread? The Body of Christ. And what do they become who partake of it? The Body of Christ: not many bodies, but one body. For as the bread consisting of many grains is made one, so that the grains nowhere appear; they exist indeed, but their difference is not seen by reason of their conjunction; so are we conjoined both with each other and with Christ: there not being one body for you, and another for your neighbor to be nourished by, but the very same for all.

John Chrysostom, 345?-407, West Syria

After thus baptizing the one who has believed and given his assent, we escort him to the place where are assembled those whom we call brethren, to offer up sincere prayers in common for ourselves, for the baptized person, and for all other persons wherever they may be, in order that, since we have found the truth, we may be deemed fit through our actions to be esteemed as good citizens and observers of the law, and thus attain eternal salvation. At the conclusion of prayers we greet one another with a kiss. Then, bread and a chalice containing wine mixed with water are presented to the one presiding over the brethren. He takes them and offers praise and glory to the Father of all, through the name of the Son and of the Holy Spirit, and he recites lengthy prayers of thanksgiving to God in the name of those to whom he granted such favors. At the end of these prayers and thanksgiving, all present express their approval by saying "Amen." This Hebrew word, "Amen," means "So be it." And when he who presides has celebrated the Eucharist, they whom we call deacons permit each one present to partake of the Eucharistic bread, and wine and water; and they carry it also to the absentees.

Justin Martyr, 100?-165? Rome

It is right, and good and joyful thing,
    always and everywhere to give thanks to you,
    Father Almighty, creator of heaven and earth.
You formed us in your image
    and breathed into us the breath of life.
When we turned away, and our love failed,
    your love remained steadfast.
You delivered us from captivity,
    made covenant to be our sovereign God,
    and spoke to us through your prophets. . . .

On the night in which he gave himself up for us,
    he took bread, gave thanks to you, broke the bread,
    gave it to his disciples, and said:
"Take, eat; this is my body which is given for you.
Do this in remembrance of me."

When the supper was over, he took the cup,
    gave thanks to you, gave it to his disciples, and said:
"Drink from this, all of you;
    this is my blood of the new covenant,
    poured out for you and for many
        for the forgiveness of sins.
Do this, as often as you drink it,
    in remembrance of me."

The Great Thanksgiving, Service of Word and Table

He was the Word that spake it;
He took the bread and brake it; And what the Word do make it,
That I believe and take it.

attributed to Queen Elizabeth, 1533-1603, England

"Christ has died. Christ is risen."
That is the eucharist:
  proclamation of the Lord's death,
  proclamation of his eternal life,
  optimism of men and women who know
that they are following,
  even amid the darkness and confusion of our history,
  the bright light of Christ,
  eternal life.

Oscar Romero, 1917-1980, El Salvador

The danger is not lest the soul should doubt whether there is any bread, but lest, by a lie, it should persuade itself that it is not hungry. It can only persuade itself of this by lying, for the reality of its hunger is not a belief, it is a certainty.

Simone Weil, 1909-1943, France

O the depth of love divine,
Th' unfathomable grace!
Who shall say how bread and wine
God into man conveys!
How the bread his flesh imparts,
How the wine transmits his blood,
Fills his faithful people's hearts
With all the life of God!

Sure and real is the grace,
The manner be unknown;
Only meet us in thy ways
And perfect us in one.
Let us taste the heavenly powers;
Lord, we ask for nothing more.
Thine to bless, 'tis only ours
To wonder and adore.

Charles Wesley, 1707-1788, England

"Lift up your hearts." "We lift them up" Ah me!
I cannot, Lord, lift up my heart to Thee:
Stoop, lift it up, that where thou art I too may be.
"Give me thy heart." I would not say Thee nay,
But have no power to keep or give away
My heart, stoop, Lord, and take it to Thyself today.

Stoop, Lord, as once before, now once anew
Stoop, Lord, and hearken, hearken, Lord, and do,
And take my will, and take my heart, and take me too.

Christina Rossetti, 1830-1894, England

Gracious Voices

Anyone who wishes to receive the Holy Sacrament must offer to God Almighty an empty, single, and hungry soul.

Therefore it is most fitting when the soul is least fit, which means, when the soul feels altogether wretched, poor, and devoid of grace, it is most receptive for God's grace and least fitted to receive it.

But then the soul must endeavour to come to the Sacrament with perfect faith, or with all the faith possible, and most firmly believing that she will receive grace. For a man receives as much as he believes he will receive. Therefore faith alone is the best and highest preparation.

Your hungry heart must build upon these words and you must trust the promise of the divine truth, and in this spirit go to the Sacrament, imploring God and saying, Lord, it is true that I am not worthy that Thou shouldst come under my roof, yet I am needy, and eager for Thy help and grace, that I too may be made godly. Thus I come with no plea but that I have heard sweet words, name-ly, that Thou dost invite me to Thy table. Dear Lord, Thy Word is true, I do not doubt it. In that faith I eat and drink with Thee. May it be done to me according to Thy Will and Words. Amen.

That is to come worthily to the Sacrament.

Martin Luther, 1483-1546, Germany

Every time the church gathers together for the Lord's Supper, it joyfully proclaims that, wonder of wonders, Jesus still chooses the same kind of sinful, disreputable dinner companions which once got him in so much trouble.

Thank God.

William Willimon, United States

All of the other kinds of eating can also take place at the Rotary Club, PTA functions, garden club meetings, gatherings sponsored by one or another political party, and social functions generally. The Eucharist, by contrast, is unique to the church. No one else has it, or should be expected to know what to do with it. It is, in fact, a part of the "strangeness" of the church.

Laurence Hull Stookey, United States

Yet I, least of all souls,
Take Him in my hand
Eat Him and drink Him,
And do with Him what I will!

Why then should I trouble myself
As to what the angels experience?

Mecthild of Magdeburg, 1212-1283, Germany

They devoted themselves to the apostles' teaching and fellow-ship, to the breaking of bread and the prayers.

Acts 2:42

How often should our church have the Lord's Supper? We might better ask, How often should we eat? . . . The Lord's Supper is the normal food for Christians. Sometimes the service is special and significant for us. Sometimes it is not. But whether a service strikes you as deeply moving or as routine, the important thing is that you are fed.

William Willimon, United States

Ritual, Symbol, Sacrament, and Sacrifice are . . . more, not less valid expressions of the Spirit of Worship, because they belong at one and the same time to the world of sense and the world of spirit: for this is the actual situation of the amphibious creature by whom these means have been devised and used.

Evelyn Underhill, 1875-1941, England

To live out the meaning of baptism propels us back to the sources of grace and courage. So, while there may be specific times of corporate reaffirmation and renewal of baptismal vows, every time we come to the table of the Lord we acknowledge and continue to grow into that which has been given by God "by water and the Spirit." To share the holy meal of the Lord's Supper presents us with a living Word, read and sung, prayed and proclaimed. Every work of mercy, each act of love, and all endeavors by the church to serve the society in which we live are such reminders. But it is the eucharistic sharing that focuses most explicitly upon the manner in which the suffering of God may transform us.

Don Saliers, United States

The day of the Lord's Supper is an occasion of joy for the Christian community. Reconciled in their hearts with God and the brethren, the congregation receives the gift of the body and blood of Jesus Christ, and, receiving that, it receives forgiveness, new life, and salvation. It is given new fellowship with God and men. The fellowship of the Lord's Supper is the superlative fulfillment of Christian fellowship. As the members of the congregation are united in body and blood at the table of the Lord so will they be together in eternity. Here the community has reached its goal. Here joy in Christ and his community is complete. The life of Christians together under the Word has reached its perfection in the sacrament.

Dietrich Bonhoeffer, 1906-1945, Germany

Gracious Voices

MINISTRY: SCATTERING TO SERVE

**By your Holy Spirit make us one
in ministry to all the world**

I am no longer my own, but thine.
Put me to what thou wilt, rank me with whom thou wilt.
Put me to doing, put me to suffering.
Let me be employed for thee or laid aside for thee,
exalted for thee or brought low by thee.
Let me be full, let me be empty.
Let me have all things, let me have nothing.
I freely and heartily yield all things
to thy pleasure and disposal.
And now, O glorious and blessed God,
Father, Son, and Holy Spirit,
thou art mine, and I am thine. So be it.
And the covenant which I have made on earth,
let it be ratified in heaven. Amen.

John Wesley's Covenant Prayer

In humble reliance upon divine grace,
  do you make it the supreme purpose of your life
  to give yourself unreservedly to the work of Christ
    in your appointed field?

Order for Commissioning Deaconesses or Missionaries

Ultimately there is only one authority for ministry. That authority is Jesus Christ. When laity claim they cannot exercise ministry in the Church because they lack authority, my immediate initial response is, "Who says?" The authority is there. It has been given in baptism. No one can take it away; no structure, no institution, no church, no clergy can take away that which is fundamental to who we are in Christ.

The authority for ministry is Jesus Christ. The Church only validates that authority and regulates it according to what seems to be needed. This is extremely important to the recovery of a sense of total ministry within the Christian Church. We are more than wanderers. We are a people under authority, engaged in a journey which leads not merely to a sense of personal wholeness, but to the wholeness of the human family. The way this journey is supported and sustained, therefore, is of crucial importance, not only for ourselves, but for the future of the planet Earth. A bold claim, yes. But unless we are bold in our vision, there is great danger that we will settle for a world or a task that is too small.

James C. Fenhagen, United States

I look upon
all the world
as my
parish.

John Wesley,
1703-1791, England

Behold, from faith thus flow forth love and joy in the Lord, and from love a joyful, willing, and free mind that serves one's neighbor willingly and takes no account of gratitude or ingratitude, of praise or blame, gain or loss.

Martin Luther, 1483-1546, Germany

When the church of Jesus shuts its outer door,
lest the roar of traffic drown the voice of prayer,
may our prayers, Lord, make us ten times more aware
that the world we banish is our Christian care.

If our hearts are lifted where devotion soars
high above this hungry, suffering world of ours,
lest our hymns should drug us to forget its needs,
forge our Christian worship into Christian deeds.

Lest the gifts we offer, money, talents, time,
serve to salve our conscience, to our secret shame,
Lord, reprove, inspire us by the way you give;
teach us, dying Savior, how true Christians live.

Fred Pratt Green, England

Scriptural holiness entails more than personal piety; love of God is always linked with love of neighbor, a passion for justice and renewal in the life of the world.

The Book of Discipline of The United Methodist Church, 1992

I will imagine that my soul and body are like two hands of a compass, and that my soul, like the stationary hand, is fixed in Jesus, who is my center, and that my body, like the moving hand, is describing a circle of assignments and obligations.

Anthony Mary Claret, 1807-1870, Spain

In one of the places in Melbourne I visited an old man and nobody ever knew that he existed. I saw his room in a terrible state, and I wanted to clean his house and he kept on saying: "I'm all right!" But I repeated the same words: "You will be more all right if you will allow me to clean your place," and in the end he allowed me. There in that room there was a beautiful lamp covered with the dirt of many years, and I asked him, "Why do you not light your lamp?" Then I asked him, "Will you light the lamp if the Sisters come to see you?" And the other day he sent me word: "Tell my friend the light she has lit in my life is still burning. Simple acts of love and care keep the light of Christ burning."

Mother Teresa of Calcutta, India

Gracious Voices

Cheap grace is the deadly enemy of our church. We are fighting today for costly grace.

Cheap grace means grace sold in the market like cheapjacks' wares. The sacraments, the forgiveness of sin, and the consolations of religion are thrown away at cut prices . . . Cheap grace is the preaching of forgiveness without requiring repentance, baptism without church discipline, Communion without confession, absolution without personal confession. Cheap grace is grace without discipleship, grace without the cross, grace without Jesus Christ, living and incarnate.

Costly grace is the treasure hidden in the field, for the sake of it a man will gladly go and sell all that he has. It is the pearl of great price to buy which the merchant will sell all his goods. It is the kingly rule of Christ, for whose sake a man will pluck out the eye which causes him to stumble, it is the call of Jesus Christ at which the disciple leaves his nets and follows him.

Costly grace is the gospel which must be *sought* again and again, the gift which must be *asked* for, the door at which a man must *knock.*

It is *costly* because it calls us to follow, and it is *grace* because it calls us to follow *Jesus Christ.* It is costly because it costs a man his life, and it is *grace* because it gives a man the only true life.

Dietrich Bonhoeffer, 1906-1945, Germany

We are going home to many who cannot read. So, Lord, make us Bibles so that those who cannot read the Book can read it in us.

prayer from China

I mean by "goal" that for the sake of which everything is done, for example: The goal of agriculture is the enjoyment of its fruits; the goal of building a house is living in it; the goal of commerce is wealth; and the goal of striving in contests is the prize. In the same way, too, the goal of the sublime way of life is being called a servant of God.

Gregory of Nyssa, 331?-394, Asia Minor

If a man may preach, because the Saviour died for him, why not the woman? seeing he died for her also. Is he not a whole Saviour, instead of a half one? as those who hold it wrong for a woman to preach, would seem to make it appear.

Did not Mary *first* preach the risen Saviour, and is not the doctrine of the resurrection the very climax of Christianity—hangs not all our hope on this, as argued by St. Paul? Then did not Mary, a woman, preach the gospel? for she preached the resurrection of the crucified Son of God.

But some will say, that Mary did not expound the Scripture, therefore, she did not preach, in the proper sense of the term. To this I reply, it may be that the term *preach,* in those primitive times, did not mean exactly what it is now *made* to mean; perhaps it was a great deal more simple then, than it is now;—if it were not, the unlearned fishermen could not have preached the gospel at all, as they had no learning.

Jarena Lee, 1783-185?, United States

A knowledge of God cannot be taught or learned apart from living out a life that is a reflection of who God is . . . Knowledge of God does not consist of a set of answers to a list of questions. It is more like the way a wife knows her husband, or a husband knows his wife. The knowledge husband and wife have of each other includes a profound respect for the otherness of the other; based in love, each seeks to preserve the integrity of the other, allowing the other to be without simply becoming an extension of the spouse. It is a knowledge that comes out of living together, responding to each other's daily interests and needs, being shaped by deep caring for the other. It is a transforming knowledge.

Roberta Bondi, United States

The heart of Christian ministry is Christ's ministry of outreaching love. Christian ministry is the expression of the mind and mission of Christ by a community of Christians that demonstrates a common life of gratitude and devotion, witness and service, celebration and discipleship.

The Book of Discipline of The United Methodist Church, 1992

A woman—seventy-three—whom I met on a boat last week listened eagerly to the story of love and grace, heard for the first time, and was drawn by its sweet influence. "It is good; I believe it." she said, "but I can't be a Christian." Later the story came that she supported herself by making "ghost money," and to become a Christian meant to give up all her "living," and the faith just born was not strong enough for that. I think that Jesus must look with such "compassion" upon such women. More and more I am coming to understand something of the wonderful tenderness and depth of his compassion. I have gone again and again recently to the story of Mark 6. of the hungry multitude and the compassionate Christ. It is such a privilege to take the bread of life from Him and pass it on to hungry hearts.

Laura Askew Haygood, 1845-1899, United States/China

Lord God, you have called your servants to ventures of which we cannot see the ending, by paths as yet untrodden, through perils unknown. Give us faith to go out with good courage, not knowing where we go, but only that your hand is leading us and your love supporting us; through Jesus Christ our Lord. Amen.

Lutheran Book of Worship

Gracious Voices

While every effort has been made to secure permission, we may have failed in a few cases to trace or contact the copyright owner. We apologize for any inadvertent oversight or error.

PAGE 7

You move us. From *The Confessions of St. Augustine,* F. J. Sheed, trans. Copyright © 1943 by Sheed and Ward. Reprinted with alterations by permission of Sheed & Ward, 115 E. Armour Blvd., Kansas City, MO 64111. Page 3.

Come, sinners, to the gospel feast, Charles Wesley. *The United Methodist Hymnal,* 339. Nashville: United Methodist Publishing House, 1989.

O Lord my God, Anselm, "The Proslogion," in *The Prayers and Meditations of St. Anselm,* trans. Sr. Benedicta Ward, SLG. Copyright © 1973 by Benedicta Ward. Used by permission of Penguin Books, Middlesex, England. Page 239-40.

The Lord pursued, attr. to Peter Julian Eymard in *The Wisdom of the Saints,* Jill Haak Adels, editor. Copyright © 1987 by Jill Haak Adels. Used with permission of Oxford University Press, New York. Page 42.

PAGE 8

Lord, you have come, Cesareo Gabarain. *The United Methodist Hymnal,* trans. © 1989, United Methodist Publishing House, Nashville, TN. Used with permission. Hymn 344.

Have you ever, From *The Hunger of the Heart* Copyright © 1992 by Ron DelBene, Herb Montgomery, and Mary Montgomery. Used by permission of Upper Room Books. Pages 19, 22.

For some time, Thérèse de Lisieux, *Story of a Soul,* trans. in *The Wisdom of the Saints,* Jill Haak Adels, editor. Copyright © 1987 by Jill Haak Adels. Used with permission of Oxford University Press, New York. Page 54.

PAGE 9

Come, all of you, Laotian Hymn. *The United Methodist Hymnal,* trans © 1989, United Methodist Publishing House. Hymn 350.

Whoever wishes, Alphonsus Liguori, *The Holy Eucharist,* The Rev. Eugene Grimm, ed. Brooklyn: Redemptorist Fathers, 1934. Page 477.

You have loved us, From *The Prayers of Kierkegaard* by Søren Kierkegaard. Perry D. LeFevre, ed. Copyright © 1956 by University of Chicago Press, 1956. Used by permission. Page 14.

I believe, O Lord, Richard Allen, "Acts of Faith," in Richard Allen, *Life Experience and Gospel Labors of the Rt. Rev. Richard Allen.* Copyright © 1983 by Abingdon Press, Nashville, Tennessee. Used by permission. Page 43.

Thou hidden love, Gerhard Tersteegen, trans. by John Wesley. *The United Methodist Hymnal,* Nashville: United Methodist Publishing House, 1989. Used with permission. Hymn 414.

Thirst for Jesus, Isaac of Nineveh, "Part I, " from *Syriac Fathers on Prayer and the Spiritual Life,* Sebastian Brock, ed. Copyright © 1987 Cistercian Publications Inc. Kalamazoo, Michigan and Spencer, Massachusetts. Used with permission. Page 248.

PAGE 10

The old men, From *Wisdom of the Desert Fathers,* Sister Benedicta Ward, ed. Copyright © 1975 Sisters of the Love of God, SLG Press, Oxford. Used with permission. Page 34.

ACKNOWLEDGMENTS

Here there begins, Jan Van Ruysbroeck, "The Spiritual Espousals," trans. in *The Wisdom of the Saints,* Jill Haak Adels, editor. Copyright © 1987 by Jill Haak Adels. Used with permission of Oxford University Press, New York. Page 34.

Grace strikes us, Paul Tillich, "You Are Accepted," in *The Shaking of the Foundations* by Paul Tillich. Copyright © 1948 by Charles Scribner's Sons, New York. Page 161.

God showed me, Julian of Norwich, *Revelations of Divine Love,* ed. by Clifton Wolters. Copyright ©1966 by Clifton Wolters. Published by Penguin Books, London. Page 68.

I am bold, Jonathan Edwards, in *The Works of Jonathan Edwards, Vol 2, Religious Affections.* John Smith, ed. Copyright © 1959, Yale University Press. Page 102.

We acknowledge God's, The Book of Discipline of the United Methodist Church, 1992. Page 45.

PAGE 11

Conscience. . . . John Wesley, "On Conscience," in *Works of John Wesley, Vol. VII.* Grand Rapids: Zondervan. Page 187.

But woe unto, François de Salignac de la Mothe Fénelon, *Christian Perfection.* Copyright © 1947 by Harper & Bros., New York. Used with permission of HarperCollins. Page 67.

The moment I, Charles de Foucauld, *Soldier of the Spirit: The Life of Charles de Foucauld,* by Michel Carrouges. Trans. in *The Wisdom of the Saints,* Jill Haak Adels, editor. Copyright © 1987 by Jill Haak Adels. Used with permission of Oxford University Press, New York. Page 43.

PAGE 12

Be free, therefore, John the Solitary, "Letter to Hesychius," from *Syriac Fathers on Prayer and the Spiritual Life,* Sebastian Brock, ed. Copyright © 1987 Cistercian Publications Inc. Kalamazoo, Michigan and Spencer, Massachusetts. Used with permission. Page 89.

The inward stirring, Jan van Ruysbroeck "The Spiritual Espousals," trans. in *A Dictionary of Religious Quotations,* Margaret Pepper, ed. © 1989 by Margaret Pepper. Published by Audré Deutsch Ltd, London. Page 239.

PAGE 13

Receive the mark, from "A Service for the Welcoming of Hearers," in *Come to the Waters* by Dan Benedict. Pages 139, 142.

Lord, I shall, Joseph the Visionary, "Prayer of Joseph the Visionary," From *Syriac Fathers on Prayer and the Spiritual Life,* Sebastian Brock, ed. Copyright © 1987 Cistercian Publications Inc. Kalamazoo, Michigan and Spencer, Massachusetts. Used with permission. Page 360.

An old man, from *Wisdom of the Desert Fathers,* Sister Benedicta Ward, ed. Copyright © 1975 Sisters of the Love of God, SLG Press, Oxford. Used with permission. Page 35.

Since, by assenting, Thomas Aquinas, *Summa Theologiae,* 2a2ae, Q. 6, art. 1, Vol 31, Blackfriar's Edition. © 1974 Blackfriar's, London. Page 166.

PAGE 14

Faith is a living, Martin Luther, "Preface to the Epistle to the Romans" in *Reformation Writings of Martin Luther Vol II: The Spirit of the Protestant Reformation,* Bertram Lee Woolf, ed. Copyright © 1956 by Lutterworth Press, Cambridge, England. Used with permission. Page 289.

Gracious Voices

Faith means, Søren Kierkegaard. Reprinted from *The Gospel of Suffering* by Søren Kierkegaard, translated by David F. Swenson and Lillian M. Swenson, copyright © 1947 Augsburg Publishing House. Used by Permission of Augsburg Fortress. Page 5.

Simple faith, John of the Cross, "Maxims and Counsels," in *Collected Works of St. John of the Cross,* Kieran Kavanaugh, OCD, and Otilio Rodriguez, OCD, trans. Copyright © 1964 by Doubleday, New York. Page 678.

Wednesday, August 10, From *The Journal and Letters of Francis Asbury,* Vol. 1. Elmer T. Clark, et al, eds. Copyright © 1958, Abingdon Press, Nashville, Tennessee. Page 124.

PAGE 15

Introduction, from Ignatius of Loyola, *The Spiritual Exercises, Literal Translation and a Contemporary Reading,* David L. Fleming, ed. Copyright © 1978 by Institute of Jesuit Sources, St. Louis, MO. Used with permission. Page 105.

Late have I loved you. From *The Confessions of St. Augustine,* F. J. Sheed, trans. Copyright © 1943 by Sheed and Ward. Reprinted with alterations by permission of Sheed & Ward, 115 E. Armour Blvd., Kansas City, MO 64111. Page 236.

Faith is different, From *Thoughts of Pascal,* Charles S. Jerram, trans. and ed. Published by Methuen and Co., London, 1901. Page 129.

PAGE 16

At first, Henri Nouwen, *Reaching Out.* Copyright © 1975 by Henri J. M. Nouwen. Published by Doubleday Press, New York. Used with permission. Page 66-7.

Where Charity and Love Prevail by Omer Westendorf and Paul Benoit. Copyright © 1960, 1961, World Library Publications, a division of J.S. Paluch Company, Inc. Schiller Park, IL 60176. All rights reserved. Used by permission.

PAGE 17

Love bade me, George Herbert, *Love,* in *Seventeenth-Century Prose and Poetry,* second ed. Alexander M. Witherspoon and Frank J. Warnke, eds. Copyright © 1929, 1946, 1957, 1963 by Harcourt, Brace, and World, Inc. Used with permission by Harcourt, Brace, Jovanovich. Page 859.

Do everything in common, From the Epistle of Ignatius to the Magnesians, 7:1b-2, trans. from Greek. *The Apostolic Fathers, Vol. 1,* Krisopp Lake, ed. Published 1912, Harvard University Press. Page 202.

Christianity is more, From Stanley Hauerwas and William H. Willimon, *Resident Aliens.* Copyright © 1989 by Abingdon Press, Nashville, Tennessee. Used with permission. Page 24.

Console yourself:, From *Thoughts of Pascal,* Charles S. Jerram, trans. and ed. Published by Methuen and Co., London, 1901. Page 211. Language modernized.

PAGE 18

It is therefore expected, From "The General Rules of the Methodist Church," in *The Book of Discipline of the United Methodist Church, 1992.* Page 72-3.

You have come, From *Prieres d'Ozawamick,* Native Canadian liturgical text, source untraced. In *With All God's People. The New Ecumenical Prayer Cycle,* John Carden, ed. Copyright © 1989 World Council of Churches, Geneva. Page 223.

Christianity is not, From Georgia Harkness, *Understanding the Christian Faith.* Copyright © 1947 Abingdon-Cokesbury Press, Nashville, Tennessee. Used with permission of Abingdon Press. Page 150.

PAGE 19

Many people seek, From *Life Together* by Dietrich Bonhoeffer. English translation copyright © 1954 by Harper & Brothers, copyright renewed 1982 by Helen S. Doberstein. Reprinted by permission of HarperCollins Publishers, Inc. Pages 76-8.

Nothing is so, From *Discourses and Sayings of Abbot Dorotheus of Gaza.* Translation by Eric Wheeler, O.S.B. Copyright © 1977 by Cistercian Publications, Inc. Kalamazoo, Michigan - Spencer, Massachusetts. Pages 251-53.

PAGE 20

As soon as, Geoffrey Chaucer, *The Canterbury Tales,* From *The Portable Chaucer* by Theodore Morrison. Copyright © 1949, renewed © 1977 by Theodore Morrison. Used by permission of Viking Penguin, a division of Penguin Books USA Inc. Page 53.

Christian life, In *God Walk. Liberation Shaping Dogmatics,* by Fredrick Herzog. Copyright © 1988 Orbis Press, Maryknoll, New York. Used with permission. Page 10.

God be in, From the Sarum Liturgy, *United Methodist Book of Worship,* No. 566. Used with permission of United Methodist Publishing House, Nashville, TN.

PAGE 21

We have this grace, John Wesley, "A Plain Account of Christian Perfection," *Works of John Wesley, Vol. II.* Grand Rapids: Zondervan. Pages 395-96.

An old man, From *Wisdom of the Desert Fathers,* Sister Benedicta Ward, ed. Copyright © 1975 Sisters of the Love of God, SLG Press, Oxford. Used with permission. Page 29.

One thing I have never understood, Lois A. Cheney, *God Is No Fool.* Copyright © 1969 Abingdon Press. Used with permission of Lois A. Cheney. Page 61.

The daring ambition, Theresa of Lisieux, *Story of a Soul,* trans. in *The Wisdom of the Saints,* Jill Haak Adels, editor. Copyright © 1987 by Jill Haak Adels. Used with permission of Oxford University Press, New York. Page 4.

PAGE 22

Q: What is Christian Perfection?, John Wesley, "Thoughts on Christian Perfection," in *Works of John Wesley, Vol XI.* Grand Rapids: Zondervan. Page 394.

This is true, Gregory of Nyssa, *Life of Moses.* Abraham J. Malherbe and Everett Ferguson, trans. and eds. Copyright © 1978 by the Missionary Society of St. Paul the Apostle in the State of New York. Used by permission of Paulist Press. Page 137.

Jesus had come, Mother Teresa of Calcutta, *Life in the Spirit,* Kathryn Spinks, ed. Copyright © 1983 by Kathryn Spinks. Used with permission of The Society for Promoting Christian Knowledge, London. Page 49-50.

I want Jesus to walk, African-American Spiritual. Adapt. *United Methodist Hymnal,* Hymn 521. Used by permission of United Methodist Publishing House, Nashville, TN.

PAGE 23

A God-seeker, James C. Fenhagen, *More Than Wanderers: Spiritual Disciplines for Christian Ministry.* Copyright © 1978 by Seabury Press, Inc. Used with permission of the author. Pages 1-3.

Not happiness, W. E. Sangster, *The Pure in Heart: A Study in Christian Sanctity.* Copyright © 1954 by Abingdon Press, Nashville. Page xi.

Our perfection, Angela of Foligno, *The Book of Blessed Angela,* trans. in *The Wisdom of the Saints,* Jill Haak Adels, editor. Copyright © 1987 by Jill Haak Adels. Used with permission of Oxford University Press, New York. Page 45.

Gracious Voices

Worship, in all its, From *Worship* by Evelyn Underhill. Copyright © 1936 by Evelyn Underhill. Published by Crossroad Publishing Company, New York. Page 3.

Grant, O Lord, John Hunter, *United Methodist Book of Worship,* No. 567. Used with permission of United Methodist Publishing House, Nashville, TN.

My prayers must meet, Gerard Manley Hopkins, "My prayers must meet a brazen heaven" in *The Poems of Gerard Manley Hopkins,* W. H. Gardner and N. H. MacKenzie, eds. Copyright © 1967 by Society of Jesus. Used by permission of Oxford University Press. Page 27.

From hence it clearly, Jonathan Edwards, "Religious Affections," in Harold P. Simonson, ed. *Selected Writings of Jonathan Edwards.* New York: Continuum Publishing Company, 1990. Used with permission. Page 165.

PAGE 25

The time of business, Brother Lawrence of the Resurrection, *Practice of the Presence of God.* Copyright © 1963 by Peter Pauper Press. Used with permission. Page 25.

Understanding is, Augustine, Tractate XXIX.6, *On the Gospel of John* (7:14-18), in *Nicene and Post-Nicene Fathers,* Vol. VII. Grand Rapids: Eerdmans.

Come, divine interpreter, Charles Wesley. *United Methodist Hymnal,* Hymn 594. Used with permission of United Methodist Publishing House, Nashville, TN.

From the cowardice, Prayer from Kenya, *United Methodist Hymnal,* No. 597. Used with permission of United Methodist Publishing House, Nashville, TN.

Toil at reading, John the Solitary, "Letter to Hesychius," in *Syriac Fathers on Prayer and the Spiritual Life.* Copyright © 1987 Cistercian Publications, Kalamazoo, Michigan and Spencer, Massachusetts. Used with permission. Page 92.

O God, drive, From *The World At One In Prayer* by Daniel J. Fleming. Copyright © 1942 by Harper & Row, Publishers, Inc. Copyright Renewed 1970. Reprinted by permission of HarperCollins Publishers, Inc. Page 102.

PAGE 26

United Methodists share, United Methodist Book of Discipline, 1992, Pages 77-8.

Blessed Lord, Contemporary Collect, Proper 28, in *The Book of Common Prayer,* 1979. Page 236.

"Praying the Scripture" From Madame Jeanne Guyon, *Experiencing the Depths of Jesus Christ.* Copyright © 1975 by The Seed Sowers, P.O. Box 285, Sargent, GA 30275, (770) 254-9442. Used with permission.

PAGE 27

Some may, perhaps, Richard Allen, "A Short Address to the Friends of Him Who Hath No Helper," in Richard Allen, *Life Experience and Gospel Labors of the Rt. Rev. Richard Allen.* Copyright © 1983 by Abingdon Press, Nashville, Tennessee. Used by permission. Pages 80-81.

A Christian, Martin Luther, "Freedom of a Christian" 1520, in *Luther's Works, Vol. 31.* Harold J. Grimm, ed. Copyright © 1957 by Fortress Press. Used with permission of Augsburg-Fortress. Page 344.

If we pray, in *Life in the Spirit,* by Mother Theresa of Calcutta. Kathryn Spinks, ed. Copyright © 1983 by Kathryn Spinks. Used with permission of Society for Promoting Christian Knowledge, London. Page 1.

PAGE 28

A man possessed, From *Wisdom of the Desert Fathers,* Sister Benedicta Ward, ed. Copyright © 1975 Sisters of the Love of God, SLG Press, Oxford. Used with permission. Page 47.

Serve your God, Glen E. Rainsley, *Touch Holiness.* © 1990 by Pilgrim Press. Used with permission. Page 241.

It was said, From *Wisdom of the Desert Fathers,* Sister Benedicta Ward, ed. Copyright © 1975 Sisters of the Love of God, SLG Press, Oxford. Used with permission. Page 59.

Do you want, John Chrysostom, Homily 50 on St. Matthew 14:23,24. Trans. in *The Wisdom of the Saints,* Jill Haak Adels, editor. Copyright © 1987 by Jill Haak Adels. Used with permission of Oxford University Press, New York. Page 15.

When we only, Isabella Thoburn, "The Law of Christian Service," in *Life of Isabella Thoburn* by Bishop J. M. Thoburn. Copyright © 1903 by Jennings and Pye, Cincinnati. Repr. 1987 by Garland Publishing, Inc. New York. Page 246.

PAGE 29

Eternal Father, Thanksgiving over the Water, Baptismal Covenant, *United Methodist Hymnal.* Page 36. Used with permission of United Methodist Publishing House, Nashville, TN.

Describe [God], The Book of Privy Counseling. Reprinted from *The Wisdom of the Saints* by Jill Haak Adels. Copyright © 1987 by Jill Haak Adels. Used with permission of Oxford University Press. Page 8.

Like the sun, From 1987 *United Methodist Clergywomen's Consultation Resource Book.* Written by Rev. Lydia S. Martinez, Page 57.

PAGE 30

The stories, Kosuke Koyama, *Fifty Meditations.* Copyright © 1975 by Christian Journals Limited. Published by Orbis Press, 1979. Used with permission. Page 13-14.

Suppose someone asked, C. S. Lewis, *Mere Christianity.* Copyright © 1943, 1945, 1952 by Macmillan Publishing Co., Inc. Used by permission of HarperCollins Publishers, Ltd, London. Page 21.

Maker, in whom, Charles Wesley. *United Methodist Hymnal,* Hymn 88. Used with permission of United Methodist Publishing House, Nashville, TN.

PAGE 31

For the first, Brother Lawrence of the Resurrection, *Practice of the Presence of God.* Copyright © 1963 by Peter Pauper Press. Used with permission. Pages 30-1.

To call God, From Theodore Jennings, *Life as Worship: Prayer and Praise in Jesus' Name.* Copyright © 1982 by Wm. B. Eerdmans Publishing Co. Grand Rapids, Michigan. Used with permission. Page 34.

God of us all, Service of Death and Resurrection, *United Methodist Hymnal,* Page 874. Used with permission of United Methodist Publishing House, Nashville, TN.

God, who stretched, Catherine Cameron. Copyright © 1967 Hope Publishing Co., Carol Stream, IL 60188. All rights reserved. Used by permission. *United Methodist Hymnal,* Hymn 150.

If you contemplate, attr. to John Eudes in *The Wisdom of the Saints* by Jill Haak Adels. Copyright © 1987 by Jill Haak Adels. Used with permission of Oxford University Press. Page 10.

Gracious Voices

Though we cannot, Anonymous, *The Cloud of Unknowing,* paraph. Ch. LXX, from *The Wisdom of the Saints* by Jill Haak Adels. Copyright © 1987 by Jill Haak Adels. Used with permission of Oxford University Press. Page 137.

PAGE 32

God is creating, Dom Robert Petitpierre, O.S.B., *Living With God.* Copyright © 1968 by Robert Petitpierre. Published by S.P.C.K. Press, London. Used with permission. Page 3.

Wherever you cast, John Calvin, *Institutes of the Christian Religion,* I.V.1. Copyright © 1960 by W. L. Jenkins. Published by The Westminster Press, Philadelphia. Pages 52-3.

The transcendence, L. Harold DeWolf, "The God Who Speaks," in *Wesleyan Theology. A Sourcebook,* edited by Thomas A. Langford. Copyright © 1984 by Labyrinth Press, Durham, N.C. Used with permission of Baker Book House, Grand Rapids, MI. Page 218.

The almighty, John Wesley, "On Predestination," in *Works of John Wesley, Vol. VI.* Grand Rapids: Zondervan. Page 230.

I sing the almighty, Isaac Watts, *United Methodist Hymnal,* Hymn 152. Used by permission of United Methodist Publishing House, Nashville, TN.

PAGE 33

God thought, Reprinted by permission of The Putnam Publishing Group from *Waiting for God* by Simone Weil. Copyright © 1951 by G. P. Putnam's Sons; Renewed © 1979 by G. P. Putnam's Sons. Page 149-150.

We assert that, United Methodist Book of Discipline, 1992. Page 65.

I would not say, Karl Barth, *Dogmatics in Outline.* Copyright © 1959 by Harper & Row. Used with permission of SCM Press, London. Page 39.

If we had only, Martin Luther, Table Talk, November 30, 1531, "Treatment of Melancholy, Despair, etc." Reprinted from *Luther's Works,* Volume 54, edited by T. G. Tappert, copyright © 1965 Fortress Press. Used by permission of Augsburg Fortress. Page 17.

There is an encompassing, Albert Outler, "The Hallowing of Life" in *Albert Outler, The Preacher,* Bob Parrot, ed. Copyright © 1988 by Abingdon Press. Used with permission. Page 87.

With God, adapt. from Irenaeus, *Against Heresies,* Bk. IV, Ch. 16, in *The Wisdom of the Saints* by Jill Haak Adels. Copyright © 1987 by Jill Haak Adels. Used with permission of Oxford University Press. Page 11.

This is our Creator, Irenaeus, *Against Heresies,* Bk. 5, Ch. XVII.1. *Ante-Nicene Fathers, Vol. I.* Grand Rapids: Wm. B. Eerdmans, 1956. Page 544. Trans. altered.

PAGE 34

O most high, Prayer of Saint Francis of Assisi for All Created Things, *United Methodist Book of Worship,* Number 507.

The bud, Galway Kinnell, "Saint Francis and the Sow" from *Mortal Acts, Mortal Words.* Copyright © 1980 by Gallway Kinnell. Reprinted by permission of Houghton Mifflin Co. All rights reserved.

PAGE 35

A Bird came down, from *The Complete Poems of Emily Dickinson,* Copyright © 1890, 1891, 1896 by Roberts Brothers, Copyright © 1914, 1918, 1919, 1924 by Martha Dickinson Bianchi. Published by Little, Brown and Company, Boston, 1927. Page 91.

You know that, From *The Violence of Love* by Archbishop Oscar Romero. Edited by James R. Brockman and Henri Nouwen. Copyright © 1988 by Chicago Province of the Society of Jesus. Reprinted by permission of HarperCollins Publishers, Inc. Page 151.

God, like a mother, C. Eric Lincoln, *United Methodist Hymnal.* Words © 1989 United Methodist Publishing House. Used with permission. Hymn 115.

God is that, Anselm, "The Proslogion," in *The Prayers and Meditations of St. Anselm,* trans. Sr. Benedicta Ward, SLG. Copyright © 1973 by Benedicta Ward. Used by permission of Penguin Books, Middlesex, England. Page 246.

PAGE 36

About noon I preached, John Wesley, *Journal,* "Tuesday 5 April 1768," *Journal of John Wesley Vol. V,* Nehemiah Churnock, ed. London: Epworth Press, 1914, rpt. 1938. Pages 253-54.

Who was Jesus? Lois A. Cheney, *God Is No Fool.* Copyright © 1969 Abingdon Press. Used with permission of Lois A. Cheney. Page 23.

When we speak, Ambrose of Milan, "Commentary on Psalm 36," *Patrologia Latina,* Vol.14. Paris: J.P. Migne, ed. 1882. Column 1048, cap 65.

As no darkness, Gregory of Nyssa Homily 5 on Ecclesiastes. Trans. in *The Wisdom of the Saints* by Jill Haak Adels. Copyright © 1987 by Jill Haak Adels. Used with permission of Oxford University Press. Pages 14-15.

PAGE 37

A mother's, From *Revelations of Divine Love* by Julian of Norwich, translated by Clifton Wolters. Copyright © Clifton Wolters, 1966. Published by Penguin Classics. Used by permission. Page 169.

I desire and choose, Ignatius of Loyola, *The Spiritual Exercises,* in *The Wisdom of the Saints* by Jill Haak Adels. Copyright © 1987 by Jill Haak Adels. Used with permission of Oxford University Press. Page 15.

Yes, of a truth, Martin Luther, "Sermon for the first Sunday in Advent, 1533." Reprinted from *Day by Day We Magnify Thee,* edited by Margarethe Steiner and Perry Scott, copyright © 1950 Muhlenberg Press. Used by permission of Augsburg Fortress. Page 1.

Meekness was the method, John Bosco, "The Use of Punishments in Salesian Houses," January 29, 1883, in *The Biographical Memoirs of St. John Bosco, Vol XVI.* Torino: Societa Editrice Internazionale, 1935. Pages 442-43.

Through Christ, Clement of Rome, First Letter to the Corinthians, Ch. 36. In *Apostolic Fathers, Vol. 1, Loeb Classical Library.* Krisopp Lake, ed. Published 1912 by Harvard University Press. Page 70.

PAGE 38

You are the overflowing, Gertrude of Helfta, *Oeuvres Spirituelles 3: Heraut,* bk. 3, ch. 65, Pierre Doyère, ed. Paris: Editions du Cerf, 1968. Pages 264-66.

The existence, Karl Barth, *Dogmatics in Outline.* Copyright © 1959 by Harper & Row. Used with permission of SCM Press, London. Page 88.

PAGE 39

For Jesus, From Theodore Jennings, *Life as Worship: Prayer and Praise in Jesus' Name.* Copyright © 1982 by Wm. B. Eerdmans Publishing Co. Grand Rapids, Michigan. Used with permission. Page 47.

The Greek, From *Pilgrim at Tinker Creek,* by Annie Dillard. Copyright © 1974 by Annie Dillard. Used with permission of HarperCollins. Page 189.

If you are, Martin Luther, From "Sermons on the Catechism," 1528, in *Luther's Works, Vol. 51,* John W. Doberstein, ed. Copyright © 1959 by Muhlenberg Press, Philadelphia. Used by permission of Augsburg-Fortress. Page 164.

Lord Jesus Christ, Desiderius Erasmus, in *For All God's People. Ecumenical Prayer Cycle,* Copyright © 1978 by World Council of Churches, Geneva. Page 97.

PAGE 40

I say that, W. E. Sangster, *Westminster Sermons, Vol. II.* Copyright © 1961 The Epworth Press, London. Used with permission. Page 42.

Lord Jesus Christ, Bonaventure, in *The Hodder Book of Christian Prayers,* Tony Castle, ed. Published by Hodder and Stoughton Ltd, 1986. Pages 40-1.

Your speech is offensive, Wilbur E. Rees, *$3.00 Worth of God,* Copyright © 1971 Judson Press, Valley Forge, PA. Used with permission of the publisher, Judson Press, 1-800-458-3766. Page 94.

PAGE 41

Sing of Mary, Words by Roland Ford Palmer, *United Methodist Hymnal,* Hymn 272. Used with permission of United Methodist Publishing House, Nashville, TN.

Moreover we proclaim, John of Damascus, *Exposition of the Orthodox Faith* 3.12. From *Nicene and Post-Nicene Fathers,* Vol. 9. New York: Charles Scribner's Sons, 1899. Pages 55-56.

Invisible in, Leo the Great, Sermon 23.2, Letter 28.3, *Nicene and Post-Nicene Fathers,* Vol. XII, pp. 133, 140. Trans. in *The Wisdom of the Saints* by Jill Haak Adels. Copyright © 1987 by Jill Haak Adels. Used with permission of Oxford University Press. Page 12.

Woman in the night, Words by Brian Wren. Copyright © 1983 by Hope Publishing Co., Carol Stream, IL 60188. All rights reserved. Used by permission. *United Methodist Hymnal,* Hymn 274.

PAGE 42

The great mystery, Henri J. M. Nouwen, *Compassion.* Co-authored by Donald P. McNeill and Douglas A. Morrison. Copyright © 1982 by the authors. Used with permission of Doubleday Publishing. Pages 27-8.

"I, Mary, Reprinted from Dorothy L. Sayers, *A Matter of Eternity.* Copyright © 1973 by Wm. B. Eerdman's. Used with permission of David Higham Associates, London. Page 49.

Here, then, Martin Luther "Sermons from the year 1533." Reprinted from *Day by Day We Magnify Thee,* edited by Margarethe Steiner and Perry Scott, copyright © 1950 Muhlenberg Press. Used by permission of Augsburg Fortress. Page 27.

The Word was, Athanasius, "Four Discourses Against the Arians" I.42. *Nicene and Post-Nicene Fathers, Vol. IV.* Grand Rapids: Wm B. Eerdmans. Page 330.

PAGE 43

The care of, Theodoret, "The Cure of Pagan Diseases," From *Drinking From the Patristic Fountain,* by Thomas Spidlik. Copyright © 1992, New City Press, London. Published in the United States by Cistercian Publications, Inc. Kalamazoo, Michigan and Spencer, Massachusetts, 1994. Page 396.

Did you ever, C. S. Lewis, "The Incarnation" Reprinted from *The Joyful Christian,* by C. S. Lewis. Copyright © 1977 Macmillan Publishing Co. Used by permission of HarperCollins Publishers, London. Pages 50-51.

PAGE 44

On one hand, From *Mixed Blessings* by Barbara Brown Taylor. Copyright © 1986 by Barbara Brown Taylor. Published by Susan Hunt Publishing, Atlanta, GA. Page 24.

From the beginning, Evelyn Underhill. From *An Anthology of The Love of God. From the Writings of Evelyn Underhill.* Rt. Rev. Lumsden Barkway, ed. Copyright © A. R. Mowbray & Co., Ltd. Used with permission of Morehouse Publishing, Wilton, CN. Page 64.

PAGE 45

Christ's obedience . . . John Wesley, "The Lord Our Righteousness," in *Works of John Wesley, Vol. V.* Grand Rapids: Zondervan. Page 237.

Lord, you are calling, From *Catherine of Siena,* Suzanne Noffke, O.P., ed. Copyright © 1980 by the Missionary Society of St. Paul the Apostle in the State of New York. Used by permission of Paulist Press. Page 229.

God created through, Reprinted by permission of The Putnam Publishing Group from *Waiting for God* by Simone Weil. Copyright © 1951 by G. P. Putnam's Sons; Renewed © 1979 by G. P. Putnam's Sons. Pages 123-4.

We are accounted, From *The Articles of Religion of the Methodist Church,* in *The Book of Discipline,* 1992, Page 60-1.

Fix your eyes, Teresa of Avila, *Interior Castle,* in *Complete Works of Teresa of Jesus, Vol. II,* E. Allison Peers, ed. London: Sheed and Ward, 1950. Page 346.

PAGE 46

Now I was, From *Grace Abounding to the Chief of Sinners* by John Bunyan. Roger Sharrock, ed. Copyright © 1962 by Oxford, at Clarendon. Used by permission of Oxford University Press. Page 80.

I danced, Words by Sydney Carter. Copyright © 1963 by Stainer & Bell Ltd. Used by permission of Hope Publishing Co., Carol Stream, IL 60188. All rights reserved. *United Methodist Hymnal,* Hymn 261.

The Word which, Kosuke Koyama, *Three Mile An Hour God.* Copyright © 1979 by Kosuke Koyama. Used with permission of Orbis Press. Pages 24-5.

PAGE 47

I was raised up, From *Dream of the Rood,* Reprinted in *Norton Anthology of English Literature, Fifth Edition.* Copyright © 1962, 1968, 1974, 1979, 1986 by W. W. Norton & Company, Inc. Pages 23-24.

Every time, Nicolas Berdyaev, *Dostoevsky.* Donald Attwater, trans. New York: Meridian Books, 1957. Page 198.

Almighty God, From *United Methodist Book of Worship,* Copyright © 1979, 1986 by Abingdon Press, © 1992 United Methodist Publishing House. Used with permission. Page 362.

Take thought now, attr. to Bonaventure in *The Wisdom of the Saints* by Jill Haak Adels. Copyright © 1987 by Jill Haak Adels. Used with permission of Oxford University Press. Page 15.

Out of love, Clement of Rome, First Letter to the Corinthians, Ch. 49.6 in *Apostolic Fathers, Vol. I, Loeb Classical Library.* Krisopp Lake, ed. Published 1912 by Harvard University Press. Pages 92, 94.

As through, Irenaeus, *Against Heresies,* Bk. 5, Ch. XVII.2. *Ante-Nicene Fathers, Vol. 1.* Grand Rapids: Wm. B. Eerdmans, 1956. Page 545.

Gracious Voices

PAGE 48

Where have, attr. to Bernard of Clairvaux in *The Wisdom of the Saints* by Jill Haak Adels. Copyright © 1987 by Jill Haak Adels. Used with permission of Oxford University Press. Page 15.

Soul of Christ, From Ignatius of Loyola, *The Spiritual Exercises, Literal Translation and a Contemporary Reading,* David L. Fleming, ed. Copyright © 1978 by Institute of Jesuit Sources, St. Louis, MO. Used with permission. Page 2.

Too often, William Willimon. From *Sunday Dinner* by William H. Willimon. Copyright © 1980 by Upper Room. Used by permission of the publisher. Pages 88-9.

To mock your reign, Words by Fred Pratt Green. Copyright © 1973 by Hope Publishing Co., Carol Stream, IL 60188. All rights reserved. Used by permission. *United Methodist Hymnal,* Hymn 285.

PAGE 49

Wilt thou love, John Donne, *Sonnet XV,* From *The Complete Poetry and Selected Prose of John Donne,* Charles Coffin, editor. Copyright © 1952 by Random House, Inc. Used with permission. Pages 252-53.

The main thing, Dorothy Day, From *Dorothy Day. Selected Writings. By Little and By Little.* Robert Ellsberg, editor. Copyright © 1983, 1992 by Robert Ellsberg and Tamar Hennessey. Used with permission of Orbis Books. Page 359.

What takes place, Karl Barth *Dogmatics in Outline.* Copyright © 1959 by Harper & Row. Used with permission of SCM Press, London. Page 116.

PAGE 50

O Christ, Prayer of Isaac of Nineveh. From *Syriac Fathers on Prayer and the Spiritual Life.* Sebastian Brock, ed. Copyright © 1987 Cistercian Publications Inc., Kalamazoo, Michigan and Spencer, Massachusetts. Used with permission. Page 353.

He breaks the power, Charles Wesley, "O For A Thousand Tounges To Sing," *United Methodist Hymnal,* Hymn 57. Used with permission of United Methodist Publishing House, Nashville, TN.

Jesus truly suffered, Cyril of Jerusalem, *Catechetical Lectures.* In *Fathers of the Church, Vol. 64.* Copyright © 1970 by The Catholic University of America Press, Washington, D.C. Used with permission. Page 6.

Fellowship with Christ, Olin A. Curtis, *The Christian Faith* published by Methodist Book Concern, 1905. Reprinted in *Wesleyan Theology. A Sourcebook,* edited by Thomas A. Langford. Copyright © 1984 by Labyrinth Press, Durham, N.C. Used with permission of Baker Book House, Grand Rapids, MI. Page 180.

By his first, Bernard of Clairvaux, *On the Love of God.* Translated by a religious of C.S.M.V. London: A. R. Mowbray and Co., Ltd., 1950. Pages 41-2.

PAGE 51

If two men, Søren Kierkegaard, "Attack Upon Christendom," in *Parables of Kierkegaard,* edited by Thomas C. Oden. Copyright © 1978 Princeton University Press. Used with permission. Pages 72-3.

Yea, truly blessed! Martin Luther, "Sermon for the Third Sunday in Advent," 1544 Reprinted from *Day by Day We Magnify Thee,* edited by Margarethe Steiner and Perry Scott, copyright © 1950 Muhlenberg Press. Used by permission of Augsburg Fortress. Page 20.

This, therefore, John Wesley, "Justification by Faith," *Works of John Wesley, Vol. V.* Grand Rapids: Zondervan. Page 359.

ACKNOWLEDGMENTS

The cup, From *On A Wild and Windy Mountain, And Twenty-Five Other Meditations for the Christian Year* by William H. Willimon. Copyright © 1984 by Abingdon Press, Nashville, TN. Used with permission. Page 72.

PAGE 52

Jesus learned obedience, Henri J. M. Nouwen. *Gracias! A Latin American Journal.* Copyright © 1983 by Henri J. M. Nouwen. Used with permission of HarperCollins. Page 183.

What one of us, Madeleine L'Engle, *The Irrational Season.* Copyright © 1977 by Crosswicks, Inc. Used with permission of HarperCollins, New York. Page 18.

It is none other, From *Life Together* by Dietrich Bonhoeffer. English translation copyright © 1954 by Harper & Brothers, copyright renewed 1982 by Helen S. Doberstein. Reprinted by permission of HarperCollins Publishers, Inc. Page 114.

PAGE 53

Christ the Lord is risen, Charles Wesley, *United Methodist Hymnal,* Hymn 302. Used with permission of United Methodist Publishing House, Nashville, TN.

How inexhaustibly rich, From *The Rising.* Copyright © 1994 by Wendy M. Wright. Used by permission of Upper Room Books. Page 118.

God did not abolish, Reprinted from Dorothy L. Sayers, *A Matter of Eternity.* Copyright © 1973 Wm. B. Eerdmans. Used with permission of David Higham Associates, London. Page 54.

PAGE 54

I look at Thee, John Henry Newman, Reprinted from *Prayers, Verses, and Devotions* by John Henry Newman. Copyright © 1989 Ignatius Press, San Francisco. All rights reserved; reprinted with permission of Ignatius Press. Page 379.

Lord, in these, from a liturgy of a Manilan slum, in *For All God's People. Ecumenical Prayer Cycle.* Copyright © 1978 World Council of Churches, Geneva. Used with permission. Page 161.

Glory to the Father, from Syrian Orthodox Liturgy. *United Methodist Book of Worship,* Number 391. Used with permission of United Methodist Publishing House, Nashville, TN.

PAGE 55

There is, Karl Barth, *Dogmatics in Outline.* Copyright © 1959 by Harper & Row. Used with permission of SCM Press, London, Page 138.

Before He entered, Cyril of Jerusalem, in *Fathers of the Church, Vol. 2.* Copyright © 1970 by The Catholic University of America Press, Washington, D.C. Used with permission. Pages 39, 50.

The New Testament, C. S. Lewis, "Miracle of the Resurrection," Reprinted from *The Joyful Christian,* by C. S. Lewis. Copyright © 1977 Macmillan Publishing Co. Used by permission of HarperCollins Publishers, London. Page 65.

PAGE 56

For a little while, A. Roy Eckardt, "Between Christmas and Good Friday." Copyright 1957 Christian Century Foundation. Reprinted by permission from the January 30, 1957 issue of *The Christian Century.*

Hail thee, festival day! Venantius Honorius Fortunatus. *United Methodist Hymnal,* Hymn 324.

The Ascension, Thomas Aquinas, *Catechetical Instructions.* Joseph B. Collins, trans. Copyright © 1939 by Joseph Wagner, New York. Page 40.

Gracious Voices

If we are, From *The Violence of Love* by Archbishop Oscar Romero. Edited by James R. Brockman and Henri Nouwen. Copyright © 1988 by Chicago Province of the Society of Jesus. Reprinted by permission of HarperCollins Publishers, Inc. Page 151.

Here then we see, John Wesley, "The End of Christ's Coming," in *The Works of John Wesley,* Vol. VI. Grand Rapids: Zondervan. Page 276.

Life and death, Thomas Merton, *No Man is an Island.* Copyright © 1955 by Abbey of Gethsemani. Used with permission of Harcourt, Brace, Jovanovich. Page 193.

I am happy, West African prayer, in *For All God's People. Ecumenical Prayer Cycle.* Copyright © 1978 by World Council of Churches. Used with permission. Page 45.

PAGE 58

The Holy Ghost, John Eudes, *Meditations on Various Subjects,* Copyright © 1947 by P. J. Kenedy & Sons. Page 77.

The Holy Ghost, From *The Articles of Religion of the Methodist Church,* In *United Methodist Book of Discipline,* 1992, Page 59.

Like the murmur, Carl P. Daw, Jr. *United Methodist Hymnal,* Hymn 544. Copyright © 1982, Hope Publishing Company.

PAGE 59

I adore thee, John Henry Newman. From *Prayers, Verses, and Devotions* by John Henry Newman. Copyright © 1989 Ignatius Press, San Francisco. All rights reserved; reprinted with permission of Ignatius Press. Page 416.

It is the Holy Spirit, Vatican Council II. Reproduced with permission from *Council Digest: The Basic Message of Vatican Council II* by Pericle Cardinal Felici, ed. Copyright © 1981 Catholic Book Publishing Co., New York, N.Y. All rights reserved. Page 56.

Christ died, Bernard of Clairvaux, Epistle 107.8, in *The Spiritual Teachings of Bernard of Clairvaux* by John R. Sommerfeldt. Copyright © 1991 Cistercian Publications, Inc. Kalamazoo, Michigan and Spencer, Massachusetts. Used with permission. Page 145.

PAGE 60

O living flame, From *John of the Cross: Selected Writings.* Copyright © 1987 by the Washington Province of Discalced Carmelite Friars, Inc. Used by permission of Paulist Press. Pgs. 293-94.

Sanctification is that, From *The Articles of Religion of the Methodist Church,* in *Book of Discipline of the United Methodist Church,* 1992, Page 65.

O Holy Ghost, attr. to Richard Rolle in *The Wisdom of the Saints* by Jill Haak Adels. Copyright © 1987 by Jill Haak Adels. Used with permission of Oxford University Press. Page 36.

PAGE 61

Come, Holy Ghost, attr. to Rhabanus Maurus, trans. by John Cosin, 1627. *United Methodist Hymnal,* Hymn 651.

The Holy Spirit's actions, Cyril of Jerusalem, Catechetical Instructions, in *Fathers of the Church,* Vol. 2. Copyright © 1970, The Catholic University of America Press, Washington, D.C. Used with permission. Page 85.

To know when, Georgia Harkness, from *The Fellowship of the Holy Spirit.* Copyright © 1966 by Abingdon Press. Used with permission. Page 99.

ACKNOWLEDGMENTS

"Life in the Spirit," From "Our Doctrinal Heritage" in *United Methodist Book of Discipline,* 1992, Page 42.

The Holy Spirit, From the Service of the Baptismal Covenant, *United Methodist Hymnal,* Page 37. Used with permission of United Methodist Publishing House, Nashville, TN.

PAGE 62

Peace of conscience, Adam Clark, *Christian Theology,* London: Thomas Tegg and Son, 1835. Reprinted in *Wesleyan Theology. A Sourcebook,* edited by Thomas A. Langford. Copyright © 1984 by Labyrinth Press, Durham, N.C. Used with permission of Baker Book House, Grand Rapids, MI. Page 44.

Who is the third, T.S. Eliot, "The Waste Land," in *Collected Poems, 1909-1935.* Copyright © 1930, 1958 by T. S. Eliot. Used by permission of Harcourt, Brace, Jovanovich. Page 87.

Will you be, From "The Order for the Ordination of Deacons," *United Methodist Book of Worship,* Copyright © 1992, United Methodist Publishing House, Nashville, TN. Used with permission. Page 666.

I'm goin' a sing, African American spiritual. *United Methodist Hymnal,* Hymn 333. Adapt. © 1989 The United Methodist Publishing House, Nashville, TN. Used with permission.

Brothers and sisters, From "A Celebration to New Beginnings in Faith," *United Methodist Book of Worship.* Copyright © 1992 by United Methodist Publishing House, Nashville, TN. Used with permission. Page 588.

PAGE 63

I believe that I, Martin Luther, *Small Catechism,* 1529. Adapted from text in *Book of Concord,* Theodore Tappert, ed. Copyright © 1959 by Fortress Press. Used with permission of Augsburg Fortress. Page 345.

O Great Spirit, Native American prayer, adapted from *United Methodist Book of Worship,* No. 487, attributed to Church Women United, 1981 World Day of Prayer materials.

We know there, From Peter Cartwright, *The Autobiography of Peter Cartwright.* Copyright © 1956, Abingdon Press, Nashville, Tennessee. Used with permission. Page 335.

The Holy Spirit, attr. to John Vianney in *The Wisdom of the Saints* by Jill Haak Adels. Copyright © 1987 by Jill Haak Adels. Used with permission of Oxford University Press. Page 36.

PAGE 64

The church is of God, From Baptismal Covenant III, *United Methodist Hymnal.* Used with permission of United Methodist Publishing House, Nashville, TN. Page 45.

The church is, Cyprian, "The Unity of the Catholic Church" in *Fathers of the Church, Vol. 36.* The Catholic University of America Press, Washington, D.C. Used with permission. Pages 99-100.

A local church, From "The Local Church" in *The United Methodist Book of Discipline, 1992,* Page 116.

PAGE 65

Usually discussion about, From Laurence Hull Stookey, *Baptism. Christ's Act in the Church.* Copyright © 1982 Abingdon Press, Nashville, Tennessee. Used with permission. Pages 29-30.

Gracious Voices

By the word, attr. to Anthony of Egypt in *The Wisdom of the Saints,* Jill Haak Adels, editor. Copyright © 1987 by Jill Haak Adels. Used with permission of Oxford University Press, New York. Page 84.

The Church of Christ, Words by Fred Pratt Green. Copyright © 1971 by Hope Publishing Co., Carol Stream, IL 60188. All rights reserved. Used by permission. *United Methodist Hymnal,* Hymn 589.

Christ has organized, Pope John Paul II, *The Way to Christ. Spiritual Exercises.* Leslie Weave, trans. Copyright © 1984 by HarperCollins. Used with permission of HarperCollins, New York. Page 74.

We do not, G. K. Chesterton, in *As I Was Saying: A Chesterton Reader* by Robert Knille, ed. Copyright © 1985 by Wm. B. Eerdman's Publishing Co., Grand Rapids, MI. Page 269.

The church is, From *Thoughts of Pascal,* Charles S. Jerram, trans. and ed. Published by Methuen and Co., London, 1901. Page 207.

PAGE 66

In [Boston], Zilpah Elaw, "Memoirs of the Life, Religious Experience, Ministerial Training, and Labors of Mrs. Elaw." In *Sisters of the Spirit,* William L. Andrews, ed. Copyright © 1986 by Indiana University Press, Bloomington, IN. Used with permission. Page 117.

Almighty and eternal, From Mass for the Unity of the Church, *Roman Missal* © 1973, International Commission on English in the Liturgy, Inc. All rights reserved. Page 1014.

Our identity, John Westerhoff III, *A Pilgrim People.* Published by Seabury Press, Minneapolis, 1984. Used by permission of the author. Page 1.

You and I, Matthew Simpson, "The Church A Place of Safety and of Praise." In *Sermons of Bishop Matthew Simpson.* George R. Crooks, ed. New York: Harper and Bros., 1885. Page 291.

PAGE 67

United Methodists, From *United Methodist Book of Discipline,* 1992, Page 40-1.

The Christian is saved, Timothy Ware, in *The Orthodox Ethos: Essays in honor of the Centenary of the Greek Orthodox Archdiocese of North and South America.* A. J. Philippou, ed. Oxford: Holywell Press, 1964. Page 143.

I am the church! Words by Richard Avery and Donald Marsh. Copyright © 1972 by Hope Publishing Co., Carol Stream, IL 60188. All rights reserved. Used by permission. *United Methodist Hymnal,* Hymn 558.

Grace was in Christ, Thomas Aquinas, *Summa Theologiae* 3a. Q. 19. art. 4. Blackfriar's Edition. © 1965, Blackfriar's, London. Page 104.

The sharing we do, From *The Rising.* Copyright © 1994 by Wendy Wright. Used by permission of Upper Room Books. Page 88-9.

The Church is, Julianus Pomerius, "The Contemplative Life," Ch. XVI. *Patrologia Latina,* Vol. 59. Page 432.

PAGE 68

I think the saints, From *The Violence of Love* by Archbishop Oscar Romero. Edited by James R. Brockman and Henri Nouwen. Copyright © 1988 by Chicago Province of the Society of Jesus. Reprinted by permission of HarperCollins Publishers, Inc. Page 199.

What life have, T.S. Eliot "The Rock," in *Collected Poems, 1909-1935.* Copyright © 1930, 1958 by T. S. Eliot. Used by permission of Harcourt, Brace, Jovanovich. Page 188.

ACKNOWLEDGMENTS

Do all you can, Maximus the Confessor, "Centuries on Charity" 4.82. From *Drinking From the Patristic Fountain,* by Thomas Spidlik. Copyright © 1992, New City Press, London. Published in the United States by Cistercian Publications, Inc. Kalamazoo, Michigan and Spencer, Massachusetts, 1994. Page 218-19.

PAGE 69

Heaven is not only, From Laurence Hull Stookey, *Eucharist. Christ's Feast With the Church.* Copyright © 1982 Abingdon Press, Nashville, Tennessee. Used with permission. Page 25.

For all the saints, Words by William W. How. *United Methodist Hymnal,* Hymn 711. Used with permission of United Methodist Publishing House, Nashville, TN.

Imagine a circle, Dorotheus of Gaza, from *Œuvres Spirituelles, Dorothée de Gaza, Sources Chrétiennes,* Vol. 92, Dom L. Regnault, Dom J. de Préville, eds. Les Editions du Cerf, 29, Paris, 1963. Page 284-87.

Receive the Word, From "An Order for the Presentation of Bibles to Children" *United Methodist Book of Worship,* Copyright © 1992 by United Methodist Publishing House, Nashville, TN. Used with permission. Page 587.

Baptism also gives, From Laurence Hull Stookey, *Baptism. Christ's Act in the Church.* Copyright © 1982 Abingdon Press, Nashville, Tennessee. Used with permission. Page 37.

All praise, Charles Wesley, *United Methodist Hymnal,* Hymn 554. Used with permission of United Methodist Publishing House, Nashville, TN.

PAGE 70

O Lord, whose, From *For All God's People: Ecumenical Prayer Cycle.* Copyright © 1978 WCC Publications, World Council of Churches, Geneva, Switzerland. Page 81.

God our Father, Roman Missal © 1973, International Commission on English in the Liturgy, Inc. All rights reserved.

I sing a song, Lesbia Scott, *United Methodist Hymnal,* Hymn 712. Used with permission of United Methodist Publishing House, Nashville, TN.

Saints never know, Wilbur E. Rees, *$3.00 Worth of God,* Copyright © 1971 Judson Press, Valley Forge, PA. Used with permission of the publisher, Judson Press, 1-800-458-3766. Page 71.

PAGE 71

Bring me to see, From *The Complete Poems of Christina Rossetti, Vol 2.* edited by R. W. Crump. Copyright © 1986 by Louisiana State University Press. Pages 289-90.

I remembered, From *Believe in Me, Sermons on the Apostles' Creed* by James A. Harnish. Copyright © 1991 by Abingdon Press. Used by permission. Page 76.

The Saints were, attr. to John Vianney in *The Wisdom of the Saints,* Jill Haak Adels, editor. Copyright © 1987 by Jill Haak Adels. Used with permission of Oxford University Press, New York. Page 4.

PAGE 72

What merit, then, Augustine. Letter 194. From *Fathers of the Church, Vol. 30.* The Catholic University of America Press, Washington, D.C. Page 313.

O Lord God, Maria Stewart, *United Methodist Book of Worship,* No. 486. Used with permission of United Methodist Publishing House, Nashville, TN.

Hear the good news, From Service of Word and Table, *United Methodist Hymnal,* Page 8. Used with permission of United Methodist Publishing House, Nashville, TN.

Gracious Voices

What happened to us, From *Life Together* by Dietrich Bonhoeffer. English translation copyright © 1954 by Harper & Brothers, copyright renewed 1982 by Helen S. Doberstein. Reprinted by permission of HarperCollins Publishers, Inc. Page 115.

PAGE 73

The word "redemption", From Georgia Harkness, *Understanding the Christian Faith.* Copyright © 1947 Abingdon-Cokesbury Press, Nashville, Tennessee. Used with permission of Abingdon Press. Page 71.

How can we sinners, Charles Wesley, *United Methodist Hymnal,* Hymn 372. Used with permission of United Methodist Publishing House, Nashville, TN.

In the evening, John Wesley, Journal entry, May 28, 1738 in *Journal of John Wesley, Standard Edition, Vol. I.* London: Epworth Press, 1938. Pages 475-76.

PAGE 74

God of all, Ruth Duck, From *Bread for the Journey,* Copyright © 1981. Used by permission of The Pilgrim Press; 700 Prospect Ave. East, Cleveland, OH 44115-1100. Page 46.

Augustine said, Defensor Grammaticus, *Book of Sparkling Sayings,* 1, 5 ff. From *Drinking From the Hidden Fountain,* by Thomas Spidlik. Copyright © 1992 by New City Press, London. Published in the United States by Cistercian Publications, Kalamazoo, Michigan and Spencer, Massachusetts. Used with permission. Page 176.

I'm sure glad, Wilbur E. Rees, *$3.00 Worth of God,* Copyright © 1971 Judson Press, Valley Forge, PA. Used with permission of the publisher, Judson Press, 1-800-458-3766. Page 22.

PAGE 75

Christians do not, From *The Liturgy of Liberation* by Theodore Jennings. Copyright © 1988 by Abingdon Press. Used with permission. Page 29.

The Lord God is, From *Gates of Prayer: The New Union Prayerbook,* Copyright © 1975 by the Central Conference of American Rabbis. Used by permission. Page 392.

We believe also, John of Damascus, *Exposition of the Orthodox Faith,* 4.27. From *Nicene and Post-Nicene Fathers,* Vol. 9. New York: Charles Scribners Sons, 1899. Page 99.

PAGE 76

As for paradise, Catherine of Genoa, "Purgation and Purgatory," in *Catherine of Genoa,* Serge Hughes, trans. Copyright © 1979 by Paulist Press. Used with permission. Page 78.

Sing low, sweet chariot, African-American spiritual. *United Methodist Hymnal,* Hymn 703. Adapt. and arr. Copyright © 1989 The United Methodist Publishing House, Nashville, TN. Used with permission.

How speak trans-human, From *The Divine Comedy* by Dante Alighieri, translated by John Ciardi. Translation copyright 1954, 1957, 1959, 1960, 1061, 1965, 1967, 1970 by the Ciardi Family Publishing Trust. Reprinted by permission of W. W. Norton & Company, Inc. Page 26.

Before us, traditional Navaho prayer, *United Methodist Book of Worship,* No. 562. Used with permission of UMPH, Nashville, TN.

PAGE 77

The Christians included, Reprinted from *I Believe in the Resurrection of the Body* by Rubem Alves, copyright © 1986 Fortress Press. Used by permission of Augsburg Fortress. Pages 7-8.

I have, Joseph Cafasso *Spiritual Exercises for the Clergy,* Meditation XV, "On Heaven." Alba: Edizioni Paoline, 1955. Page 277.

PAGE 78

Although the mystery, Reproduced with permission from *Council Digest: The Basic Message of Vatican Council II* by Pericle Cardinal Felici, ed. Copyright © 1981 Catholic Book Publishing Co., New York, N.Y. All rights reserved. Page 36.

Will He not, Augustine *City of God,* Book XXII. 24 Trans. in *The Wisdom of the Saints,* Jill Haak Adels, editor. Copyright © 1987 by Jill Haak Adels. Used with permission of Oxford University Press, New York. Page 200.

It is not said, attr. to Robert Bellarmine in *The Wisdom of the Saints,* Jill Haak Adels, editor. Copyright © 1987 by Jill Haak Adels. Used with permission of Oxford University Press, New York. Page 200.

Heaven is not, attr. to Bonaventure in *The Wisdom of the Saints,* Jill Haak Adels, editor. Copyright © 1987 by Jill Haak Adels. Used with permission of Oxford University Press, New York. Page 210.

Now listen to, Meister Eckhart, Sermon 86, Luke 10:38, in *Meister Eckhart: Teacher and Preacher.* Bernard McGinn, et al, eds. Copyright © 1986, Paulist Press. Page 341.

Suppose the ocean, John Wesley, "On Eternity" in *Works of John Wesley, Vol. 2.* Copyright © 1985. Abingdon Press, Nashville, TN. Used with permission. Page 365.

PAGE 79

I remember one, Madeleine L'Engle, *The Irrational Season.* Copyright © 1977 by Crosswicks. Used with permission of HarperCollins, New York. Page 58-9.

Everyman: What desireth, From *Everyman,* in *Norton Anthology of World Masterpieces, Fifth Edition.* Vol. 1. Copyright © 1956, 1965, 1973, 1979, 1985 by W. W. Norton and Co., New York and London. Used with permission. Page 1503.

Oh! what a beautiful, African American spiritual, *Songs of Zion, Supplemental Worship Resource 12.* Copyright © 1981, 1982 by Abingdon Press, Nashville, TN. Used with permission. Hymn 169.

God must, Pierre Teilhard de Chardin, *The Divine Milieu,* Copyright © 1960 by William Collins and Sons, Ltd., London and Harper and Row, New York. Page 89.

PAGE 80

Absolute peace, Hildegard of Bingen, *Hildegardis Scivias,* edited by A. Führkotter and A. Carlevaris. *Corpus Christianorum Continuatio Mediaeualis XLIII,* Vol. 2, 1978, Pt. 3c. 12, ff. Pages 611-613. See also Emilie Zum Brunn & Georgette Epiney-Burgard, *Women Mystics in Medieval Europe.* New York: Paragon House, 1989. Page 35.

In anticipation, Anonymous, *The Cloud of Unknowing,* Ch. 48. In *The Wisdom of the Saints,* Jill Haak Adels, editor. Copyright © 1987 by Jill Haak Adels. Used with permission of Oxford University Press, New York. Page 188.

This world is not, from *The Complete Poems of Emily Dickinson,* Copyright © 1890, 1891, 1896 by Roberts Brothers, Copyright © 1914, 1918, 1919, 1924 by Martha Dickinson Bianchi. Published by Little, Brown and Company, Boston, 1927.Page 226.

Death, be not, John Donne, Sonnet X, From *The Complete Poetry and Selected Prose of John Donne,* Charles Coffin, editor. Copyright © 1978 Random House, Inc. Used with permission. Page 250-51.

Steal away, African-American Spiritual, Adapt, Arr: The United Methodist Publishing House. *United Methodist Hymnal,* Hymn 704.

Gracious Voices

Say, "Abba. From *God on Earth: The Lord's Prayer for Our Time.* Text by Will Campbell; photographs by Will McBride; poetry by Bonnie Campbell. Text and poems copyright © 1983 by Will Campbell and Bonnie Campbell. Photographs copyright © 1983 by Will McBride. Used with permission of The Crossroad Publishing Company, New York. Page 7.

God, Who stands, Evelyn Underhill From *An Anthology of The Love of God. From the Writings of Evelyn Underhill.* Rt. Rev. Lumsden Barkway, ed. Copyright © A. R. Mowbray & Co., Ltd. Used with permission of Morehouse Publishing, Wilton, CN. Page 46.

For me, prayer, Therese de Lisieux, *Story of a Soul,* trans. in *The Wisdom of the Saints,* Jill Haak Adels, editor. Copyright © 1987 by Jill Haak Adels. Used with permission of Oxford University Press, New York. Page 37.

I repeat, Pope John XXIII, from *The Dorothy Day Book.* Templegate Publishers, Springfield, Ill. Page 100.

PAGE 82

The care the eagle, R. Deane Postlethwaite, *United Methodist Hymnal,* Hymn 118. Used with permission.

I have always, From *Praying Through The Lord's Prayer.* Copyright © 1992 by Steve Harper. Used by permission of Upper Room Books. Page 72.

We may observe, John Wesley, "Sermon on the Mount VI," in *John Wesley's Fifty-Three Sermons,* Edward H. Sugden, ed. Published by Abingdon Press, 1983. Page 315.

I do not, William Willimon. From *Remember Who You Are* by William H. Willimon. Copyright © 1980 by The Upper Room. Used by permission of the publisher. Page 41.

PAGE 83

In prayer one drinks, Bernard of Clairvaux, "Sermon on Song of Songs," 18.5. in *The Spiritual Teachings of St. Bernard,* translation by John R. Sommerfeldt. Copyright © 1991 Cistercian Publications Inc. Kalamazoo, Michigan and Spencer Massachusetts. Page 196.

On what basis, From Theodore Jennings, *Life as Worship: Prayer and Praise in Jesus' Name.* Copyright © 1982 by Wm. B. Eerdmans Publishing Co. Grand Rapids, Michigan. Used with permission. Page 35.

Our Father., John Wesley, "Sermon on the Mount VI," in *John Wesley's Fifty-Three Sermons,* Edward H. Sugden, ed. Published by Abingdon Press, 1983. Page 316.

I don't say, attr. to old peasant of Ars in *The Wisdom of the Saints,* Jill Haak Adels, editor. Copyright © 1987 by Jill Haak Adels. Used with permission of Oxford University Press, New York. Page 37.

PAGE 84

Regarding "Who art, Gregory of Nyssa, "On the Lord's Prayer." From *Drinking From the Hidden Fountain* by Thomas Spidlik. Copyright © 1992 New City Press, London. Published in the United States by Cistercian Publications, Inc. Kalamazoo, Michigan and Spencer, Massachusetts, 1994. Pages 345-6.

Give us, Señor, From the United Church Board for World Ministries "Calendar of Prayer, 1986-1987." Used with permission. Page 53.

My words fly up, William Shakespeare, *Hamlet,* Act 3, Scene 3. In *Shakespeare. Four Tragedies.* David Bevington, ed. Copyright © 1988 by Bantam Books, New York. Page 111.

ACKNOWLEDGMENTS

PAGE 85

What is the meaning, Origen, *On Prayer,* 24.1. From *Drinking From the Hidden Fountain* by Thomas Spidlik. Copyright © 1992 New City Press, London. Published in the United States by Cistercian Publications, Inc. Kalamazoo, Michigan and Spencer, Massachusetts, 1994. Page 346-47.

The love of God, From *Revelations of Divine Love* by Julian of Norwich, translated by Clifton Wolters. Copyright © Clifton Wolters, 1966. Used by permission of Penguin Publishing Co., New York. Pages 70-71.

Enable me, Susanna Wesley, in *The Prayers of Susanna Wesley.* W. L. Doughty, ed. New York: Philosophical Library, 1956. Page 31.

You can't, Mark Twain (Samuel Langhorne Clemens) *The Adventures of Huckleberry Finn.* Copyright © 1884 by Samuel L. Clemens. © 1896, 1899 by Harper & Bros., 1912 by Clara Gabrilowitch, 1923 by Mark Twain Co., 1940 by Heritage Press, New York. Chapter XXXI title.

PAGE 86

The feelings, Bernard of Clairvaux, "Sermon on the Song of Songs," 67.3. Translation adapted by John R. Sommerfeldt, *The Spiritual Teachings of Bernard of Clairvaux.* Copyright © 1991 Cistercian Publications Inc. Kalamazoo, Michigan and Spencer Massachusetts. Used with permission. Page 215.

All our life, Clement of Alexandria "The Stromata," Bk. VII, ch. 7 in *Ante-Nicene Fathers, Vol. II.* Grand Rapids: Wm. B. Eerdmans. Page 533.

Holy, holy, holy, Great Thanksgiving *Sanctus,* Service of Word and Table, *United Methodist Hymnal,* Page 9. A Service of Word and Table I, Copyright © 1972, 1980, 1985, 1989, UMPH.

We can, however, Reprinted by permission of The Putnam Publishing Group from *Waiting for God* by Simone Weil. Copyright © 1951 by G. P. Putnam's Sons; Renewed © 1979 by G. P. Putnam's Sons. Pages 214-15.

PAGE 87

"The kingdom of God, Origen, *On Prayer,* 25. From *Drinking From the Patristic Fountain,* by Thomas Spidlik. Copyright © 1992, New City Press, London. Published in the United States by Cistercian Publications, Inc. Kalamazoo, Michigan and Spencer, Massachusetts, 1994. Pages 347-48.

For the kingdom, John Wesley, *Explanatory Notes Upon the New Testament,* Romans 14:17. London: Epworth Publishing, 1954. Page 575.

Try hard to, Catherine of Siena "Letter to certain monasteries of Bologna." Translation by Suzanne Noffke, O.P. Used with her permission.

PAGE 88

Where now are, John Chrysostom, Homily 1 on Eutropius, trans. in *The Wisdom of the Saints,* Jill Haak Adels, editor. Copyright © 1987 by Jill Haak Adels. Used with permission of Oxford University Press, New York. Page 25.

One day my mother, Julia A. J. Foote "Brand Plucked From the Fire" in *Sisters of the Spirit,* William L. Andrews, ed. Copyright © 1986 Indiana University Press, Bloomington, IN. Used with permission of the publisher. Page 167.

However, prayer is, Reprinted with the permission of Scribner, a Division of Simon and Schuster from *Man's Quest for God* by Abraham Joshua Heschel. Copyright (c) 1954 by Abraham Joshua Heschel, Renewed 1982 by Hannah Susannah Heschel and Sylvia Heschel. Page 8.

Gracious Voices

The central meaning, From Georgia Harkness, *Understanding the Christian Faith.* Copyright © 1947 Abingdon-Cokesbury Press, Nashville, Tennessee. Used with permission of Abingdon Press. Pages 159-60.

Thy kingdom come, Martin Luther, "Exposition of the Lord's Prayer for simple layfolk." Reprinted from *Day by Day We Magnify Thee,* edited by Margarethe Steiner and Perry Scott, copyright © 1950 Muhlenberg Press. Used by permission of Augsburg Fortress. Page 10.

When Israel was, African American Spiritual, in *United Methodist Hymnal,* Hymn 448. Copyright © 1989 UMPH.

PAGE 90

Lord, make me, Prayer of St. Francis of Assisi, *United Methodist Hymnal,* Number 481.

Help me, Lord, Susanna Wesley, in *The Prayers of Susanna Wesley.* W. L. Doughty, ed. New York: Philosophical Library, 1956. Page 15.

PAGE 91

O day of peace, Words by Carl P. Daw, Jr. Copyright © 1982 by Hope Publishing Co., Carol Stream, IL 60188. All rights reserved. Used by permission. *United Methodist Hymnal,* Hymn 729.

The Coming of the Kingdom, Evelyn Underhill From *An Anthology of The Love of God. From the Writings of Evelyn Underhill.* Rt. Rev. Lumsden Barkway, ed. Copyright © A. R. Mowbray & Co., Ltd. Used with permission of Morehouse-Barlow Co., Inc., Wilton, CN. Page 73.

Some people glorify, William Willimon. From *Remember Who You Are* by William H. Willimon. Copyright © 1980 by The Upper Room. Used by permission of the publisher. Page 37.

PAGE 92

We who are, Origen, *On Prayer,* 26.1. From *Drinking From the Patristic Fountain,* by Thomas Spidlik. Copyright © 1992, New City Press, London. Published in the United States by Cistercian Publications, Inc. Kalamazoo, Michigan and Spencer, Massachusetts, 1994. Page 349.

Pray that the Lord, Evagrius, *Sentences on Prayer,* 479 ff. From *Drinking From the Patristic Fountain,* by Thomas Spidlik. Copyright © 1992, New City Press, London. Published in the United States by Cistercian Publications, Inc. Kalamazoo, Michigan and Spencer, Massachusetts, 1994. Page 368.

Lord, grant us, Lucy Rider Meyer, in *High Adventure: Life of Lucy Rider Meyer* by Isabelle Horton. Copyright © 1928 by Isabelle Horton. Published by The Methodist Book Concern. Pages 273-74.

PAGE 93

My ego is, Howard Thurman. From *Conversations With God* by James Melvin Washington. Copyright © 1994 by James Melvin Washington. Reprinted by permission of HarperCollins Publishers, Inc. Page 182.

When therefore, John Wesley, "Sermon on the Mount VI," in *John Wesley's Fifty-Three Sermons,* Edward H. Sugden, ed. Published by Abingdon Press, 1983. Page 320.

Wearing our straw, From *The World At One In Prayer* by Daniel J. Fleming. Copyright © 1942 by Harper & Row, Publishers, Inc. Copyright Renewed 1970. Reprinted by permission of HarperCollins Publishers, Inc. Page 44.

ACKNOWLEDGMENTS

PAGE 94

If we are not, John Calvin, *The Golden Book of the True Christian Life.* Copyright © 1952 by Baker Book House. Used with permission. Pages 22-3.

Therefore with mind, attr. to Bede the Venerable in *The Wisdom of the Saints,* Jill Haak Adels, editor. Copyright © 1987 by Jill Haak Adels. Used with permission of Oxford University Press, New York. Page 46.

There is, perhaps, Hannah Whitall Smith, *The Christian's Secret of a Happy Life,* New York: Fleming Revel Co., 1888, 1916. Page 186.

PAGE 95

And indeed nothing, adapt. from William Law, *A Serious Call to a Devout and Holy Life - The Spirit of Love.* Paul G. Stanwood, ed. Copyright © 1978 by the Missionary Society of St. Paul the Apostle in the State of New York. Used by permission of Paulist Press. Pages 49-50.

People say, Martin Luther, "Exposition of the Lord's Prayer for simple lay-folk." Reprinted from *Day by Day We Magnify Thee,* edited by Margarethe Steiner and Perry Scott, copyright © 1950 Muhlenberg Press. Used by permission of Augsburg Fortress. Page 86.

Lord Jesus, From *The World At One In Prayer* by Daniel J. Fleming. Copyright © 1942 by Harper & Row, Publishers, Inc. Copyright Renewed 1970. Reprinted by permission of HarperCollins Publishers, Inc. Page 97.

PAGE 96

Certain monks, a saying of the Desert Fathers, From *Drinking From the Patristic Fountain,* by Thomas Spidlik. Copyright © 1992, New City Press, London. Published in the United States by Cistercian Publications, Inc. Kalamazoo, Michigan and Spencer, Massachusetts, 1994. Page 287.

By "bread", John Wesley, "Sermon on the Mount VI," in *John Wesley's Fifty-Three Sermons,* Edward H. Sugden, ed. Published by Abingdon Press, 1983. Pages 320-21.

Community is also, Peter Walpot "True Yieldedness and the Christian Community of Goods" in *Early Anabaptist Spirituality,* William L. Andrews, ed. Copyright © 1978 by the Missionary Society of St. Paul the Apostle in the State of New York. Used by permission of Paulist Press. Pages 146-47.

PAGE 97

Bread represents life, Gregory of Nyssa, On the Lord's Prayer. From *Drinking From the Patristic Fountain,* by Thomas Spidlik. Copyright © 1992, New City Press, London. Published in the United States by Cistercian Publications, Inc. Kalamazoo, Michigan and Spencer, Massachusetts, 1994. Page 350.

When I started, From Peter Cartwright, *The Autobiography of Peter Cartwright.* Copyright © 1956, Abingdon Press, Nashville, Tennessee. Used with permission. Page 338.

"Our Father, . . . From *God on Earth: The Lord's Prayer for Our Time.* Text by Will Campbell; photographs by Will McBride; poetry by Bonnie Campbell. Text and poems copyright © 1983 by Will Campbell and Bonnie Campbell. Photographs copyright © 1983 by Will McBride. Used with permission of The Crossroad Publishing Company, New York. Page 40.

Give what, Augustine, *Confessions,* 10. XXIX, F. J. Sheed, trans. Copyright © 1943 by Sheed and Ward, New York. Page 237. Used by permission with modifications.

PAGE 98

Abba Gregory, John Moschos, *The Spiritual Meadow,* translation by John Wortley. Copyright © 1992 by Cistercian Publications Inc. Kalamazoo, Michigan and Spencer, Massachusetts. Page 143.

Gracious Voices

Be present, John Cennick, *United Methodist Hymnal,* Hymn 621.

In [a second, Thomas Aquinas, *Catechetical Instructions,* Joseph B. Collins, trans. Copyright © 1939 by Joseph Wagner, New York. Page 158.

Make us worthy, Mother Teresa of Calcutta, *United Methodist Hymnal,* Number 446.

PAGE 99

An old man, From *Wisdom of the Desert Fathers,* Sister Benedicta Ward, ed. Copyright © 1975 Sisters of the Love of God, SLG Press, Oxford. Used with permission. Page 42.

What, after all, From Theodore Jennings, *Life as Worship: Prayer and Praise in Jesus' Name.* Copyright © 1982 by Wm. B. Eerdmans Publishing Co. Grand Rapids, Michigan. Used with permission. Page 49.

Gain all, John Wesley, "The Use of Money," in *John Wesley's Fifty-Three Sermons,* Edward H. Sugden, ed. Published by Abingdon Press, 1983. Page 636, ff.

PAGE 100

Almighty and most merciful God, Prayer of Confession, *United Methodist Hymnal,* Number 891.

Augustine said, Defensor Grammaticus, *Book of Sparkling Sayings,* 5. From *Drinking From the Patristic Fountain,* by Thomas Spidlik. Copyright © 1992, New City Press, London. Published in the United States by Cistercian Publications, Inc. Kalamazoo, Michigan and Spencer, Massachusetts, 1994. Page 231.

FORGIVE US, Fridoline Ukur, in *For All God's People. Ecumenical Prayer Cycle.* Copyright © 1978 by World Council of Churches. Used with permission of the Christian Conference of Asia. Page 165.

PAGE 101

Don't ever hurt, Maximus the Confessor, *Centuries on Charity,* 4.32. From *Drinking From the Patristic Fountain,* by Thomas Spidlik. Copyright © 1992, New City Press, London. Published in the United States by Cistercian Publications, Inc. Kalamazoo, Michigan and Spencer, Massachusetts, 1994. Pages 233-34.

Do not cause, From the *Letter of Barnabas,* in *Fathers of the Church, Vol. 1.* The Catholic University of America Press, Washington, D.C. Used with permission. Pages 220-21.

If we are, John Wesley, Preface to "The Doctrine of Original Sin," *Works of John Wesley, Vol. IX.* Grand Rapids: Zondervan Publishing Co. Page 194.

The work of purging, Francis de Sales, *Introduction to the Devout Life,* John K. Ryan, ed. Copyright © 1950, 1952, 1966 by John K. Ryan. Published by Doubleday Press. Page 48.

Only one, William Temple, *Personal Religion and The Life of Fellowship,* Published by Longman, Green, and Co., New York. N.D. Page 46.

PAGE 102

The mercy of God, Cassian, *Conferences,* 9.22. From *Drinking From the Patristic Fountain,* by Thomas Spidlik. Copyright © 1992, New City Press, London. Published in the United States by Cistercian Publications, Inc. Kalamazoo, Michigan and Spencer, Massachusetts, 1994. Page 351.

The more we learn, From *Life Together* by Dietrich Bonhoeffer. English translation copyright © 1954 by Harper & Brothers, copyright renewed 1982 by Helen S. Doberstein. Reprinted by permission of HarperCollins Publishers, Inc. Pages 106-07.

ACKNOWLEDGMENTS

PAGE 103

And if any, John Wesley, "A Plain Account of Christian Perfection," in *Works of John Wesley,* Vol. XI. Grand Rapids: Zondervan Publishing Co. Page 435.

And on the Lord's, From the *Didache,* in *Fathers of the Church,* Vol.1. The Catholic University of America Press, Washington, D.C. Used with permission. Page 182.

Lonely the boat, Helen Kim. *United Methodist Hymnal,* Hymn 476. Used by permission of United Methodist Publishing House, Nashville, TN.

The treasures, Anne Bradstreet, *Works of Anne Bradstreet,* Jeannie Hensley, ed. Published by Belknap Press of Harvard University, 1967. Copyright © 1967 by President and Fellows of Harvard College. Page 282.

An old man, From *Wisdom of the Desert Fathers,* Sister Benedicta Ward, ed. Copyright © 1975 Sisters of the Love of God, SLG Press, Oxford. Used with permission. Page 29.

PAGE 104

If a man, From *Discourses and Sayings of Abbot Dorotheus of Gaza.* Translation by Eric Wheeler, O.S.B. Copyright © 1977 by Cistercian Publications, Inc. Kalamazoo, Michigan - Spencer, Massachusetts. Pages 251-53.

The request, Cassian, *Conferences,* 9.23. From *Drinking From the Patristic Fountain,* by Thomas Spidlik. Copyright © 1992, New City Press, London. Published in the United States by Cistercian Publications, Inc. Kalamazoo, Michigan and Spencer, Massachusetts, 1994. Page 352.

So great are, John of the Cross, Prologue, *Ascent of Mt. Carmel,* in *Complete Works of St. John of the Cross,* E. Allison Peers, trans. © 1935, 1953, Burns and Oates, Ltd. Page 11.

But it may, John Wesley, "The End of Christ's Coming," *Works of John Wesley, Vol. VI.* Grand Rapids: Zondervan Publishing Co. Page 275.

PAGE 105

The Lord's Prayer, Cyprian, *On the Lord's Prayer.* From *Drinking From the Patristic Fountain,* by Thomas Spidlik. Copyright © 1992, New City Press, London. Published in the United States by Cistercian Publications, Inc. Kalamazoo, Michigan and Spencer, Massachusetts, 1994. Page 353.

Deliver us from, From *God on Earth: The Lord's Prayer for Our Time.* Text by Will Campbell; photographs by Will McBride; poetry by Bonnie Campbell. Text and poems copyright © 1983 by Will Campbell and Bonnie Campbell. Photographs copyright © 1983 by Will McBride. Used with permission of The Crossroad Publishing Company, New York. Page 64.

You should not, Isaac of Nineveh, "Centuries on Knowledge," in *Syriac Fathers on Prayer and the Spiritual Life,* Sebastian Broack, ed. Copyright © 1987 Cistercian Publications, Kalamazoo, Michigan and Spencer Massachusetts. Used with permission. Page 264.

An old man said, From *Wisdom of the Desert Fathers,* Sister Benedicta Ward, ed. Copyright © 1975 Sisters of the Love of God, SLG Press, Oxford. Used with permission. Page 51.

Gracious Voices

PAGE 106

One of the saints, John Moschos, *The Spiritual Meadow,* translation by John Wortley. Copyright © 1992 by Cistercian Publications Inc. Kalamazoo, Michigan and Spencer, Massachusetts. Page 188.

He taught us, From *God on Earth: The Lord's Prayer for Our Time.* Text by Will Campbell; photographs by Will McBride; poetry by Bonnie Campbell. Text and poems copyright © 1983 by Will Campbell and Bonnie Campbell. Photographs copyright © 1983 by Will McBride. Used with permission of The Crossroad Publishing Company, New York. Pages 64-5.

The human heart, Martin Luther, "Preface to the Psalms," 1528, in *Reformation Writings of Martin Luther Vol II: The Spirit of the Protestant Reformation,* Bertram Lee Woolf, ed. Copyright © 1956 by Lutterworth Press, Cambridge, England. Used with permission. Page 269.

PAGE 107

Two old men, From *Wisdom of the Desert Fathers,* Sister Benedicta Ward, ed. Copyright © 1975 Sisters of the Love of God, SLG Press, Oxford. Used with permission. Page 60.

O thou, from whom, attr. to Augustine, *For All God's People. An Ecumenical Prayer Cycle.* Copyright © 1978 by World Council of Churches. Page 21.

Precious Lord, Thomas A. Dorsey, *United Methodist Hymnal,* Hymn 474. Used with permission of Unichappell Music, Inc. c/o Hal Leonard Publishing Corp; PO Box 13819; Milwaukee, WI 53213.

Almighty and everlasting, from A Service of Healing I, in *United Methodist Book of Worship.* Copyright © 1992 UMPH, Nashville, TN. Used with permission. Pages 616, 621.

An old man, From *Wisdom of the Desert Fathers,* Sister Benedicta Ward, ed. Copyright © 1975 Sisters of the Love of God, SLG Press, Oxford. Used with permission. Page 48.

PAGE 108

We are dependent, Jonathan Edwards, "God Glorified in Man's Dependence," in Harold P. Simonson, ed. *Selected Writings of Jonathan Edwards.* New York: Continuum Publishing Company, 1990. Used with permission. Page 52.

Immortal, invisible, Walter C. Smith, in *United Methodist Hymnal,* Hymn 103.

Yea, Amen! Charles Wesley, "Lo, He Comes with Clouds Descending," in *United Methodist Hymnal,* Hymn 718.

It happened that, Søren Kierkegaard, "Either/Or," in *Parables of Kierkegaard,* edited by Thomas C. Oden. Copyright © 1978 Princeton University Press. Used with permission. Page 3.

PAGE 109

O Consuming Fire, From *The Complete Works of Elizabeth of the Trinity, Volume One* Translated by Sr. Aletheia Kane, O.C.D. copyright © 1984 by Washington Province of Discalced Carmelites, Inc. ICS Publications 2131 Lincoln Road, N.E. Washington, D.C. Pages 183-84.

Just as Moses, Bernard of Clairvaux, "Sermon on Song of Songs," 45.1 From *The Spiritual Teachings of Bernard of Clairvaux* by John R. Sommerfeldt. Copyright © 1991 Cistercian Publications, Inc. Kalamazoo, Michigan and Spencer, Massachusetts. Page 220.

To God be, Fanny J. Crosby, in *United Methodist Hymnal,* Hymn 98.

The first ideas, Anthony Mary Claret, *Autobiography of Anthony Mary Claret.* Translation from *The Wisdom of the Saints,* Jill Haak Adels, editor. Copyright © 1987 by Jill Haak Adels. Used with permission of Oxford University Press, New York. Page 29.

How swiftly, Thomas à Kempis, *Imitation of Christ,* E. M. Blaiklock, ed. Copyright © 1978 by Thomas Nelson Publishers, Nashville, TN. Used with permission.

PAGE 110

O burning Mountain, Mecthild of Magdeburg, *United Methodist Hymnal,* Number 104.

Almighty God, Susanna Wesley, in *Prayers of Susanna Wesley.* W. L. Doughty, ed. New York: Philosophical Library, 1956. Page 21.

Hath any man, Jonathan Edwards, "God Glorified in Man's Dependence," in Harold P. Simonson, ed. *Selected Writings of Jonathan Edwards.* New York: Continuum Publishing Company, 1990. Used with permission. Page 64.

A life of faith, Henri Nouwen, *Show Me the Way* : Readings for Each Day of Lent. Copyright © 1992 by Henri J. M. Nouwen. Based on *Zeige mit der Weg: Text für alle Tage von Aschermittwoch bis Ostern,* edited by Franz Johna. (C) Verlag Herder Freiburg im Breisgau 1990. Used with permission of The Crossroad Publishing Company, New York. Page 15.

PAGE 111

You are standing, Cyril of Jerusalem, *Catechesis* 3.3, in *Fathers of the Church, Vol. 63.* The Catholic University of America Press, Washington, D.C. Used with permission, translation modified. Pages 109-10.

Baptism is, John Wesley, "Treatise on Baptism," 1756, in *The Works of John Wesley,* Vol. X. Grand Rapids: Zondervan. Page 188.

Wash, O God, Ruth Duck, in *United Methodist Hymnal,* Hymn 605. Copyright © 1989 UMPH.

Pour out your, Thanksgiving Over the Water, Baptismal Covenant I, *United Methodist Hymnal,* Page 36. Copyright © 1976, 1980, 1985, 1989, UMPH. Used with permission.

PAGE 112

Therefore, O blessed, Tertullian, *On Baptism,* translated from the Latin in *Tertullian's Homily on Baptism,* Ernest Evans, ed. © 1964 S.P.C.K., London. Page 42.

My teenage daughter, from "Rechley Clad" by Gail Ramshaw, *Weavings,* Vol. XI, No. 1, January/February 1996. Copyright © 1996 by Upper Room Books. Used with permission of the author. Pages 29, 32.

The strange, Cyril of Jerusalem, Mystagogical Lecture, 2.5, in *Fathers of the Church, Vol. 64.* The Catholic University of America Press, Washington, D.C. Used with permission. Page 165.

PAGE 113

Therefore, baptism, Hans Hut, "On the Mystery of Baptism. Baptism as Symbol and as Essence, the Beginning of a True Christian Life. John 5" 1526, in *Early Anabaptist Spirituality,* Daniel Liechty, ed. Copyright © 1994 by Daniel Liechty. Used by permission of Paulist Press. Page 78.

In the midst, William Willimon. From *Remember Who You Are* by William H. Willimon. Copyright © 1980 by The Upper Room. Used by permission of the publisher. Pages 60-1.

I have come, C. S. Lewis, *The Pilgrim's Regress* Published by Eerdman's, Grand Rapids, MI. Copyright © 1933, 1943 by C. S. Lewis. Used with permission of HarperCollins, London. Page 168.

PAGE 114

The persons, Zilpha Elaw, "Memoirs of the Life, Religious Experience, Ministerial Training, and Labors of Mrs. Elaw." In *Sisters of the Spirit,* William L. Andrews, ed.. Copyright © 1986 by Indiana University Press, Bloomington, IN. Pages 60-1.

Gracious Voices

Among the local taverns, "The Baptism of Jesse Taylor" written by Dallas Frazier and Sanger D. Shafer. Copyright © 1972 by Acuff-Rose Music Inc. All Rights Reserved. Used by Permission.

PAGE 115

So when I, Theodore of Mopsuestia, Catechetical Homily, 3.5. In *The Awe-Inspiring Rites of Initiation* by Edward Yarnold, S.J. Copyright © 1971 by St. Paul Publications, Slough, England. Page 192.

Thus the person, Martin Luther, "Sermon on the holy and venerable Sacrament of Holy Baptism," 1519. Reprinted from *Day by Day We Magnify Thee,* edited by Margarethe Steiner and Perry Scott, copyright © 1950 Muhlenberg Press. Used by permission of Augsburg Fortress. Page 275.

Now is the moment, Ignatius of Antioch, Epistle to the Romans 5:3-6:1, trans. from *The Apostolic Fathers, Vol. 1,* Krisopp Lake, ed. Published 1912, Harvard University Press. Page 232.

PAGE 116

Christ is being baptized, in *Holy the Firm,* by Annie Dillard. Copyright © 1977 by Annie Dillard. Used with permission of HarperCollins Publishers, New York. Pages 66-8.

Ritual action has, From Laurence Hull Stookey, *Baptism. Christ's Act in the Church.* Copyright © 1982 Abingdon Press, Nashville, Tennessee. Used with permission. Page 26.

PAGE 117

The sign is, From Laurence Hull Stookey, *Baptism. Christ's Act in the Church.* Copyright © 1982 Abingdon Press, Nashville, Tennessee. Used with permission. Page 26.

When we are baptized, From Stanley Hauerwas and William H. Willimon, *Resident Aliens.* Copyright © 1989 by Abingdon Press, Nashville, Tennessee. Used with permission. Page 52.

Christians are the, Dom Robert Petitpierre, O.S.B., *Living With God.* Copyright © 1968 by Robert Petitpierre. Published by S.P.C.K. Press, London. Pages 21, 22.

PAGE 118

To remember our baptism, in *Worship and Spirituality,* by Don E. Saliers. Copyright © 1984 by Don E. Saliers. Published by Westminster Press, Philadelphia. Used by permission of Don E. Saliers. Page 62.

What does being baptized, John Chrysostom, *Homily X,* on Romans 5:12. In *Nicene-Post Nicene Fathers,* Vol. 2, Published by Eerdman's Press, Grand Rapids, MI. N.D. Used with permission. Pages 405-06.

PAGE 119

Batter my heart, John Donne, Sonnet XIV, From *The Complete Poetry and Selected Prose of John Donne,* Charles Coffin, editor. Copyright © 1952 by Random House, Inc. Used with permission. Page 252.

The preacher, from Flannery O'Connor, "The River" in *A Good Man Is Hard to Find and Other Stories,* copyright © 1953 by Flannery O'Connor and renewed 1981 by Regina O'Connor. Reprinted with permission of Harcourt Brace, Jovanovich. Pages 39-41.

ACKNOWLEDGMENTS

PAGE 120

As a woman, adapt. from John Chrysostom Baptismal Homily III. tran. in *The Wisdom of the Saints,* Jill Haak Adels, editor. Copyright © 1987 by Jill Haak Adels. Used with permission of Oxford University Press, New York. Page 81.

O Thou who, Charles Wesley, *United Methodist Hymnal,* Hymn 613.

Whenever you receive, Henri J. M. Nouwen, *Letters to Marc.* Copyright © 1987, 1988 by Henri J. M. Nouwen. English translation copyright © 1988 by Harper & Row, Publishers, Inc. and Darton, Longman & Todd Ltd. Reprinted by permission of HarperCollins Publishers and Gill and Macmillan Publishers, Dublin. Page 58.

I believe, Richard Allen, "Acts of Faith," in Richard Allen, *Life Experience and Gospel Labors of the Rt. Rev. Richard Allen.* Copyright © 1983 by Abingdon Press, Nashville, Tennessee. Used by permission. Pages 42-43.

Father of earth and heaven, Charles Wesley, From The Love Feast Liturgy, Copyright © 1992, UMPH. Used with permission. *United Methodist Book of Worship,* Page 583.

PAGE 121

Now the Silence, Words by Jaroslav J. Vajda. Copyright © 1969 by Hope Publishing Co., Carol Stream, IL 60188. All rights reserved. Used by permission. *United Methodist Hymnal,* Hymn 619.

The Lord's Supper, Karl Barth, *Dogmatics in Outline.* Copyright © 1959 by Harper & Row. Used with permission of SCM Press, London. Page 155.

In fact, Reprinted by permission of The Putnam Publishing Group from *Waiting for God* by Simone Weil. Copyright © 1951 by G. P. Putnam's Sons; Renewed © 1979 by G. P. Putnam's Sons. Page 214.

PAGE 122

With Thine Image, From "The Offering of the New Law, The One Oblation Once Offered." In *The Complete Poems of Christina Rossetti,* Vol. III, edited by R. W. Crump. Copyright © 1990 by Louisiana State University Press. Reprinted by permission of Louisiana State University Press. Page 29.

Sanctify me, Prayer of Isaac of Nineveh. From *Syriac Fathers on Prayer and the Spiritual Life,* Sebastian Brock, ed. Copyright © 1987 Cistercian Publications Inc., Kalamazoo, Michigan and Spencer, Massachusetts. Used with permission. Page 351.

For we, who, John Chrysostom, *Homily XXIV* on I Cor. 10:13, From *Nicene and Post-Nicene Fathers,* Vol. 12. Published in 1989 by Wm. B. Eerdmans, Grand Rapids, Michigan. Used with permission. Page 140.

PAGE 123

After thus baptizing, Justin Martyr, "First Apology" Ch. 65, in *The Fathers of the Church, Vol. 6,* The Catholic University of America Press, Washington, D.C. Reprinted with permission. Pages 104-05.

It is right, From The Great Thanksgiving, *Service of Word and Table I,* Copyright © 1972, 1980, 1985, 1989, UMPH. Used with permission. *United Methodist Hymnal,* Page 9.

He was the Word, attributed to Queen Elizabeth I in *The Holy State and The Profane State,* Vol. II, by Thomas Fuller, 1642. Maximilian Graff Walton, ed. Published 1938 by Columbia University Press, New York. Page 315.

PAGE 124

"Christ has died., From *The Violence of Love* by Archbishop Oscar Romero. Edited by James R. Brockman and Henri Nouwen. Copyright © 1988 by Chicago Province of the Society of Jesus. Reprinted by permission of HarperCollins Publishers, Inc. Page 167.

Gracious Voices

The danger is not, Reprinted by permission of The Putnam Publishing Group from *Waiting for God* by Simone Weil. Copyright © 1951 by G. P. Putnam's Sons; Renewed © 1979 by G. P. Putnam's Sons. Page 210.

O the depth, Charles Wesley, *United Methodist Hymnal,* Hymn 627.

"Lift up your hearts." "Sursum Corda," From *The Complete Poems of Christina Rossetti,* Vol. II, edited by R. W. Crump. Copyright © 1990 by Louisiana State University Press. Reprinted by permission of Louisiana State University Press. Pages 311-12.

PAGE 125

Anyone who wishes, Martin Luther, "Sermon on the worthy reception of the holy and true Body of Christ." Reprinted from *Day by Day We Magnify Thee,* edited by Mararethe Steiner and Perry Scott, copyright © 1950 Muhlenberg Press. Used by permission of Augsburg Fortress. Page 163.

Every time, William Willimon. From *Sunday Dinner* by William H. Willimon. Copyright © 1981 by The Upper Room. Used by permission of the publisher. Page 52.

All of the other, From Laurence Hull Stookey, *Eucharist. Christ's Feast With the Church.* Copyright © 1982 Abingdon Press, Nashville, Tennessee. Used with permission. Page 104.

Yet I, least, Mechtild of Magdeburg, From *The Revelations of Mechtild of Magdeburg,* Lucy Menzies, ed. Copyright © 1953 by Longmans, Green & Co. Used by permission of Random House, Inc. Page 48.

PAGE 126

How often, William Willimon. From *Sunday Dinner* by William H. Willimon. Copyright © 1981 by The Upper Room. Used by permission of the publisher. Pages 99-100.

Ritual, Symbol, Evelyn Underhill, *Worship.* Copyright © 1936 by Evelyn Underhill. Used with permission of Crossroad Publishing, New York. Page 24.

To live out the meaning, in *Worship and Spirituality,* by Don E. Saliers. Copyright © 1984 by Don E. Saliers. Published by Westminster Press, Philadelphia. Used by permission of Don E. Saliers. Page 75.

The day of the Lord's Supper, From *Life Together* by Dietrich Bonhoeffer. English translation copyright © 1954 by Harper & Brothers, copyright renewed 1982 by Helen S. Doberstein. Reprinted by permission of HarperCollins Publishers, Inc. Page 122.

PAGE 127

I am no longer, Covenant Prayer in the Wesleyan Tradition. United Methodist Hymnal, No. 607. Used with permission of UMPH.

In humble reliance, From Order for Commissioning to the Office of Deaconesses or Missionaries II, Copyright © 1964, 1965 by Board of Publication of The Methodist Church, Inc.; renewal © 1971, 1972 by Abingdon Press; © 1992 UMPH; renewal © 1992 UMPH. In *United Methodist Book of Worship,* Page 742.

Ultimately there is, James C. Fenhagen, *More Than Wanderers: Spiritual Disciplines for Christian Ministry.* Copyright © 1978 by Seabury Press, Inc. Used with permission of the author. Pages 14-15.

PAGE 128

Behold, from faith, Martin Luther, "Freedom of a Christian" in *Luther's Works, Vol. 31.* Helmut T. Lehman, ed. Copyright © 1960 by Muhlenberg Press. Used with permission of Augsburg-Fortress.

ACKNOWLEDGMENTS

When the Church, Words by Fred Pratt Green. Copyright © 1969 by Hope Publishing Co., Carol Stream, IL 60188. All rights reserved. Used by permission. *United Methodist Hymnal,* Hymn 592.

Scriptural holiness, in *United Methodist Book of Discipline,* 1992, Page 46.

I will imagine, Anthony Mary Claret, "The Temple and Palace of our Master," Prologue, in *San Antonio Maria Claret. Escritos espirituales,* Padre Jesus Bermejo, ed. Madrid: B.A.C., 1985. Page 147. Translation from *The Wisdom of the Saints,* Jill Haak Adels, editor. Copyright © 1987 by Jill Haak Adels. Used with permission of Oxford University Press, New York. Page 16.

In one of the places, in *Life in the Spirit,* by Mother Theresa of Calcutta. Kathryn Spinks, ed. Copyright © 1983 by Kathryn Spinks. Used with permission of Society for Promoting Christian Knowledge, London. Pages 40-1.

PAGE 129

Cheap grace, Dietrich Bonhoeffer, *The Cost of Discipleship.* Second edition, Copyright © SCM Press Ltd, 1959. Used with permission. Pages 45, 47.

I mean by "goal", From *Life of Moses,* by Gregory of Nyssa. Abraham Malherbe and Everett Ferguson, trans. and eds. Copyright © 1978 by the Missionary Society of St. Paul the Apostle in the State of New York. Used by permission of Paulist Press. Page 136.

If a man may preach, Jarena Lee, "The Life and Religious Experience of Jarena Lee," from *Sisters of the Spirit,* William L. Andrews, ed. Copyright © 1986 Indiana University Press, Bloomington, IN. Used with permission of the publisher. Pages 36-7.

We are going, From *The World At One In Prayer* by Daniel J. Fleming. Copyright © 1942 by Harper & Row, Publishers, Inc. Copyright Renewed 1970. Reprinted by permission of HarperCollins Publishers, Inc. Page 43.

PAGE 130

A knowledge of, Reprinted from *To Love as God Loves* by Roberta Bondi, copyright © 1987 Fortress Press. Used by permission of Augsburg Fortress. Page 101.

The heart of Christian, in *United Methodist Book of Discipline,* 1992, Page 109.

[A] woman, Laura Askew Haygood, in Oswald E. Brown, and Anna M. Brown, *Life and Letters of Laura Askew Haygood.* Nashville: Publishing House of the Methodist-Episcopal Church, South, 1904. Page 381.

Lord God, you have called, concluding collect, Evening Prayer, in *Lutheran Book of Worship.* Copyright © 1978 by Lutheran Church in America, The American Lutheran Church, The Evangelical Lutheran Church of Canada, The Lutheran Church-Missouri Synod. Published by Augsburg Publishing House, Minneapolis. Page 153.

Gracious Voices